THE LIFE AND TIMES OF
MICK JONES

THE LIFE AND TIMES OF
MICK JONES

David Saffer

TEMPUS

Mick would like to dedicate this book to his wife Glenis, daughter Lindsey and son Mark.

First published 2002

PUBLISHED IN THE UNITED KINGDOM BY:
Tempus Publishing Ltd
The Mill, Brimscombe Port
Stroud, Gloucestershire GL5 2QG

PUBLISHED IN THE UNITED STATES OF AMERICA BY:
Tempus Publishing Inc.
2 Cumberland Street
Charleston, SC 29401

British Library Cataloguing in Publication Data.
A catalogue record for this book is available from the British Library.

ISBN 0 7524 2419 X

Typesetting and origination by Tempus Publishing.
Printed in Great Britain by Midway Colour Print, Wiltshire

CONTENTS

PREFACE

It seems incredible to think that twenty-seven years have passed since I retired as a player. All I ever wanted to be was a footballer, and of course thousands of boys had the same dream as me but only a few made it.

I could not have had a better apprenticeship than at Sheffield United in the 1960s, because the club was geared to developing their team from the junior side, and indeed many of us made our Division One debuts whilst still teenagers. During five years, I finished as the top scorer on three occasions and represented England at under-23 and full international level.

When Leeds United paid a club record fee of £100,000 for me in 1967, I joined a team that was on the threshold of becoming one of the greatest sides of post-war football. Working under Don Revie, I won all my major honours.

Naturally, I have many wonderful memories, and some painful ones too, but for me the greatest thrill was playing week in week out with the likes of Billy Bremner, Norman Hunter, John Giles and Allan Clarke. Even though I had to retire early, football had been good to me. I travelled all over the world, played with and against many of the greatest players of the 1960s and '70s, and achieved all my playing ambitions.

When David approached me about writing my biography, I had no hesitation in giving him my permission. Having known David for many years, I knew it would be researched thoroughly so I could recall in detail all the key moments from my days as a player with Sheffield United, Leeds United and England. He has also made sure that it is profusely illustrated and statistically accurate.

I would like to thank all the people who have contributed, especially Sir Geoff Hurst for his kind words in the foreword. Geoff and I, both being front players, rarely came across each other during matches, but my team-mates always told me what a handful he was to play against, and of course his hat-trick in the 1966 World Cup final is one of English football's finest moments.

Putting this book together has been extremely enjoyable and has brought back fantastic memories. I hope it does for you too.

Mick Jones

INTRODUCTION

The first time I saw Leeds United play was in the Fairs Cup final against Ferencvaros in August 1968. Being only eight years old at the time, I can't recall all the action, but I have never forgotten the moment Leeds scored. The noise in the ground was deafening, the joy and exhilaration incredible.

To me the number nine's tap-in was the greatest goal I'd ever seen. I was hooked not only on Leeds United but I also had a hero… the goal scorer Mick Jones. For six years there would be many more magical moments as Leeds United took on all-comers at home and abroad, becoming the most consistent team in England and one of the most feared outfits in European football.

My favourite football memory… that's easy, the FA Cup final in 1972. 'Sniffer' Clarke scored the goal, but Mick was just as much a hero when he bravely walked across the Wembley pitch, arm strapped to his body, to meet the Queen. That moment is twinned with the memory of the winning goal itself – which of course Mick created.

Mick Jones led the line, and was ably supported by his striking-partner Clarke. Backing them up were Bremner, Giles, Charlton, Hunter, Lorimer…

Of course, there was so much more to Mick's career. A hero to thousands of Sheffield United fans and an England international who played with many of the boys of '66. For a decade, Mick played with and against all the greats of the 1960s and '70s, but more of that in the coming pages.

I've been privileged that Mick has shared his memories with me, and would like to thank all the individuals who have given their time to enable me to write his biography, especially Sir Geoff Hurst for providing the foreword. When a player with Sir Geoff's reputation says that Mick 'was one of the very best of his era', you begin to understand how highly Mick was regarded.

A legend in two football cities – Mick Jones was some player.

Enjoy the memories.

David Saffer
August 2002

FOREWORD

My abiding memory of Mick Jones is of a hunched figure, with his arm in a sling, walking up the steps to the Royal Box at Wembley to collect his FA Cup winners' medal in 1972. It was an emotional moment for him, and for Leeds United. They had won the FA Cup at last and, dislocated elbow or not, Mick wanted to enjoy every moment of the day.

Mick Jones, of course, is remembered for far more than his role that day in the Centenary FA Cup Final and I was delighted when given the chance to acknowledge his contribution to the game in this foreword. As a striker myself I was able to appreciate all the qualities Mick brought to Leeds United when Don Revie signed him from Sheffield United in September 1967. As I recall the fee at the time was £100,000. In today's transfer market he would be worth millions.

When Mick arrived at Elland Road, Revie was in the process of building a team. When he retired eight years later Revie had established Leeds as one of the greatest club sides of the past-war years. Mick had played a significant part in a rise that took them from the backwaters of the Second Division to the European Cup final in the space of eleven years. For a good part of that time, he and Allan Clarke were the most feared striking partnership in the old First Division. 'Sniffer' Clarke joined the club from Leicester City in 1969 and immediately benefited from Mick's power and physical presence. I always thought 'Sniffer' was at his best when hunting for goals in the formidable shadow of Mick Jones. They were a tremendous combination and, along with Peter Lorimer, gave Leeds awesome goalscoring potential.

It was a team of stars – Charlton, Hunter, Cooper, Bremner, Giles etc – and in that kind of environment it's possible that Mick didn't always get the recognition he deserved. I thought he was a key component in their line-up, strong, brave and the man who provided the entire team with an attacking focal point. I know myself just how tough it was in those days to lead the line. Defenders were allowed to tackle from behind, from above, from beneath, from the side, in fact from anywhere. There would have been many days when Mick Jones collapsed in the dressing room at the end of a match covered in cuts and bruises.

Like me, he spent much of each match with his back to the opposition goal. This meant that he took a regular battering from the opposing defenders. Like me, I'm sure he feels that we would both have thrived in the modern game. Rule changes have given forward players far greater protection than we received in the sixties and seventies.

As it was, Mick enjoyed an enormously successful career at club level with Leeds, winning the Football League Championship and old Fairs Cup twice, in addition to the FA Cup. He was also a beaten finalist in the Cup-Winners' Cup and twice in the FA Cup. I wish I had experienced as much success in my own club career, although I do remember a couple of cherished moments against Leeds United. It says much for the team's reputation at the time that I still recall the delight I felt at beating them.

Mick will remember the day in 1972 when West Ham won at Elland Road as he was playing. In fact, all the big names were in the team that we beat 1-0 in a League Cup third round replay. The fact that we won at Elland Road made that occasion particularly memorable. However, my own favourite Leeds United recollection dates back to November 1966, a year before Mick joined Leeds, when I scored a hat-trick in a 7-0 win over Leeds in the League Cup at Upton Park. I was on a rich goal run at the time having scored four against Fulham the previous Saturday. I finished that season with 41 goals. Wonderful memories!

That was, of course, the season that followed England's World Cup triumph. Mick very nearly joined his club mate Jack Charlton in Sir Alf Ramsey's squad. He was a regular England under-23 international and made his senior debut before me on the summer tour of 1965. He played twice – against West Germany and Sweden – but didn't get another England cap until he faced Holland at Wembley in January 1970. On that occasion he was in the England line-up with his Leeds colleagues Norman Hunter, Terry Cooper and Jack Charlton. I remember the game particularly because I was a substitute and replaced him in the second half.

Mick was in Alf's original party of 40 players for the defence of the World Cup in Mexico that summer but didn't make it to the final 22. He was perhaps a little unlucky to be around at a time when the game was littered with high-class goalscorers like Bobby Charlton, Jimmy Greaves, Allan Clarke, Francis Lee, Jeff Astle, Joe Royle and Peter Osgood. However, I'm sure that we in the goalscorer's trade union would all agree that Mick Jones was one of the very best of his era.

Sir Geoff Hurst

ACKNOWLEDGEMENTS

I would like to thank the following people and organisations for their help with this publication. Sir Geoff Hurst; Mike Fisher and David Hartshorne at *Yorkshire Post Newspapers Ltd*; Denis Clarebrough, Sheffield United's club historian; Tony Lazenby and Phil Beeton; the *Sheffield Telegraph*; the *Worksop Guardian*; Jack Hickes Photographers; and James Howarth and Becky Gadd at Tempus Publishing Ltd.

The majority of images in this book have been supplied by *Yorkshire Post Newspapers Ltd*. In addition, every effort has been made to identify the original source of other illustrations, and where possible all quotations have been acknowledged.

1

FOOTBALL CRAZY
1945-60

Mick Jones was born in the village of Rhodesia, near Worksop, on 24 April 1945. An only child, the Jones family moved to Shireoaks, also near Worksop, where Mick spent his formative years.

My earliest memories are of the community spirit within the small mining village where I grew up. Virtually all the locals, including my dad, worked at Steetley Colliery three miles away. Although times were hard for most people, including my parents, Mum and Dad made sure I never missed out. Dad was a miner throughout his working life; Mum, like many women of her generation, looked after the house.

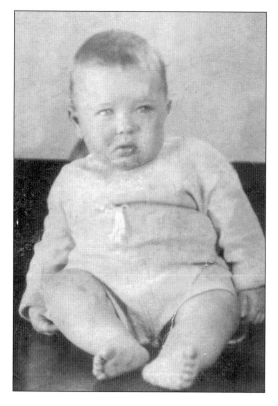

Bouncing babe, 1945.

Football was in my blood. Dad had been a goalkeeper with Worksop Town just before World War Two, and took me to games from an early age. The first Sheffield Wednesday match I went to, their centre forward Derek Dooley scored. I was six at the time and from that day on I was hooked. I loved the atmosphere of a match day and always wore my team's colours. At Christmas I'd always get something football related, whether it was a new ball or a pair of boots.

Sheffield Wednesday may have been my team, but Dad was an avid Sheffield United fan, as his father was. We used to follow Sheffield Wednesday one week,

Mick with his parents on a family holiday in Bridlington, 1948.

Sheffield United the next. My hero was Derek Dooley, who I've got to know since as a friend; he's a great character. In 1951/52 Wednesday won the Second Division title and had some great players in their side. Dooley led the line but I also marvelled at the skills of Sewell, Finney, and Quixall, and McIntosh in goal. Tragically, Derek's career was cut short following a horrific injury against Preston North End. In 1952/53 United won the title to join Wednesday in Division One. During the season they scored a stack of goals. Jimmy Hagan was the star, but he was well supported by Ringstead, Brook and Browning.

With both teams playing top-flight football, I was able to see all the stars of that era: Stanley Matthews, Tom Finney, Duncan Edwards, Nat Lofthouse, the Busby babes, you can go on and on, but for me the greatest player of all was John Charles, who played for Leeds United. I saw him play at centre-half and centre forward; he was unbelievable. I remember one game, when he was playing in defence, he had a shot from the halfway line which hit the crossbar. I couldn't believe it.

Charles was world class in both positions and proved it when he starred for Juventus. For me, he is the best all-round British player there has ever been. The number of goals he scored was phenomenal. At Leeds his goal-scoring record speaks for itself, but when you consider the number of goals he scored during his five years in Italy, where marking's so tight, that shows his calibre. As with Derek, I've been fortunate to know John for many years.

We had a field nearby our home where I used to kick a ball about until 10.30 p.m. On other occasions I'd practice outside our house for hours with a tennis ball till Mum or Dad came out to get me. I've always believed that you're born to be something. I was going to be a footballer; it meant everything to me. I wasn't interested in messing around on the street; I just wanted someone to knock a football around with.

Sheffield Wednesday, Second Division champions, 1951/52. From left to right, back row: Gannon, Curtis, Turton, McIntosh, Bannister, Whitcombe. Front row: Froggatt, Sewell, Dooley, Quixall, Rickett.

Sheffield United, Second Division champions, 1952/53. From left to right, back row: Furniss, J. Shaw, Burgin, Latham, Toner, G. Shaw. Front row: Freeman (manager), Ringstead, Hagan, Browning, Brook, Hawksworth, Jackson (trainer).

Dad saw something in me from a very young age and continually encouraged me. On many occasions he would get on his scooter and we'd go on a long run. I'd get back absolutely shattered, but it certainly built up my stamina. My parents were naturally proud of everything I eventually achieved, but whereas Dad watched me in every game, Mum got nervous and only watched the big games.

My first school was Shireoaks Junior School; I was soon in their football team. One of the teachers, Mr Cope, was coach; he was so encouraging. I started out as a centre half and he made me team captain. We played all the local teams in the Worksop area and did quite well, winning a few trophies. At eleven I had to find a new school. Dad told me there was only one school for football and that was Priory Secondary Modern, also in Worksop. Priory had a tremendous reputation for football, so I was delighted when I got a place.

I was never bothered about any of the academic subjects; all that mattered to me was Wednesday afternoons when we played all types of sport. I quickly made an impression during football trials and got into the first team, but not at centre half. Mr Curtis coached the football team and soon noticed that I was always going forward during a game trying to score goals. He moved me into attack for a match against Bentick School and it's a game I'll never forget, because I scored fourteen goals, seven in each half!

Shireoaks Junior School football team, 1955/56. Mick is holding the ball.

Time for action, 1958.

Priory School intermediate football team, 1957/58. Mick is seen third from left, front row.

Priory School senior football team, 1959/60. Mick is seen fourth from left, front row.

Bring 'em on, 1960.

At school I represented Worksop Boys. Our captain was Maurice Bembridge, who went on to make his name as a professional golfer. I then gained selection for Nottinghamshire Boys. My striking-partner was David Pleat, who was easily the best schoolboy footballer I'd seen. Against Northamptonshire Boys, David scored four goals in our 6-0 win. He was brilliant and went on to play for England schoolboys. On our way to play Derbyshire Boys one day, I remember him telling us all that Arsenal and Liverpool were after him, which didn't surprise me because he had so much talent. Eventually he joined Nottingham Forest, but he didn't make it at the top level, though he made his name as a top-flight manager.

In 1957/58 we reached the Worksop Schools final. The match was played at Worksop Town's ground where Priory faced Sir Edmund Hillary's school. I scored all our goals in a 7-0 win. The following day at school assembly the headmaster called me out to the front; I was so embarrassed! Priory was the best side in the town and my years there were brilliant. My whole life revolved around football because I was still following the exploits of Wednesday and United on alternate Saturdays. Since gaining promotion both teams had suffered relegation, though Wednesday had bounced back again in 1955/56. It was certainly never dull!

When I was fourteen Mr Curtis arranged a trial at West Brom (he knew their manager Gordon Clark) for a couple of players from our side. The match was against young apprentices who were a few years older than we were; they were also much fitter and faster. We failed to impress. Nobody doubted that we had talent, and Mr Curtis did his best to get us an extended trial to see how regular training would develop us, but it never came to anything. I was disappointed it hadn't worked out, but still believed one day I'd break into the big-time.

2
THE BREAKTHROUGH
1961-63

It was clear to everyone in Mike's life that as his school days came to an end he was only ever going to enter one profession… football. Even though only a few boys made it to the very top of the sport, Mick was determined. First, however, he had to be spotted.

I left school at fifteen and began work at Carlton Cycles in Worksop. I worked in their cycle factory as a sprayer, but wasn't playing regular football. After a few months I was having a chat with one of the lads, I told him I'd been pretty useful as a schoolboy but wasn't currently playing for anyone. He suggested I play for his team, Dinnington Miners' Welfare. Training was twice a week and they played in the Hatchard League, which was a good standard. I played against much older players than myself, and scored a hatful of goals. Suddenly, Jackie Touckay, who was a scout for Sheffield United, spotted me. He asked my dad if I would go to Bramall Lane to train; of course I would.

An official letter arrived for Mick's father on 8 February 1961 from the chief scout at Sheffield United, Archie Clark. 'Your boy's name has been forwarded to me, regarding trials with my club, should you wish it. He can come any Tuesday and Thursday evening to have training bringing what kit he has including a towel, and we will look after him and see that he gets the right coaching.'

Mick clearly impressed. On 25 February 1961 another letter arrived, this time from Sheffield United's manager, John Harris. 'I am pleased to say that it will be possible for Michael to continue training on Tuesday and Thursday evenings for the next few weeks. This will give Michael the opportunity, which we wish him to have, and I hope that he can come up to the expectations of us all. He is a nice boy, and I would like to see him get on, and it would give me much satisfaction to be able to help in Michael's future career as a Sheffield United player.'

After a few training sessions I played in a trial match at Bramall Lane. It was a big chance for me; I was determined to do well. To walk out on the pitch at fifteen and play in a match was an amazing feeling. The floodlights were on; there was only the manager, trainers and scouts looking for talent. Before the game George Smith,

Sheffield's coach, asked me where I played, I told him up front. He told me to line up alongside Les Moore in attack. The game went well for me, we won 6-4 and I scored four goals.

As I was walking off the pitch, dripping with sweat, I noticed a lot of commotion going on between John Harris, Archie Clark and the other coaches on the sidelines. Archie Clark came over, 'Where do you work son?' I told him. He said, 'You won't be working there next week, we want you to join our ground staff as an apprentice professional.' John Harris told me he'd have a word with my boss at work. I was stunned and ecstatic.

On 28 March 1961, Mick Jones joined the ground staff at Sheffield United before signing as an apprentice professional seven days later.

My first wage was £5 a week, which was a pay rise because I was on £1 11s at the cycle factory, but I didn't think about the money, I'd had my greatest wish granted, a chance to become a professional footballer. On my first day I had to arrive at 9 a.m.; the professionals arrived at 10 a.m. I expected to go in, play football and train. Life was not quite like that!

On arrival I was instructed to report to the head groundsman. He quickly explained his duties: looking after the kit, the changing rooms and the laundry, he also looked after the boiler. I was told to get a shovel and fill it. After an hour, we got changed and went out training with the first and second teams. Following a two-hour session, we had a lunch break before sweeping the terraces, cleaning the boots and collecting the dirty kits for the laundry. I quickly realised what life as an apprentice was like.

A few days later I was initiated. A few of the lads threw me in a skip, covered me with boot polish before throwing me under a shower in the changing rooms. I soon got my own back! It didn't bother me because it was all part of building the camaraderie at the club. Our training ground was three miles from Bramall Lane at the top of a steep hill. John Harris used to make us run behind his car to the top; we were shattered by the time we got there. After training we ran back down the hill, which was much more enjoyable. It was some regime, but it soon got you fit.

There was tremendous talent at the club, with the likes of Len Badger, Ken Mallender, Garth Lee, Mick Ash and the Wagstaffe brothers, Barry and Tony, serving apprenticeships. Tony became my best friend. When we both got married a few years later we were each other's best man. They were great times; we all had the same aim and encouraged each other. The atmosphere at the club was terrific because by the end of the season the first team had gained promotion back to Division One.

During the close season, Sheffield United's juniors took part in an international youth tournament in Gronigen, Holland, which attracted several Dutch and West German

Apprentice days, 1961.

teams. The team played four matches (twenty minutes each way) in one day, winning all four games. Archie Clark, who was instrumental in bringing the club's rich crop of youngsters together, took a squad of sixteen players on the trip.

Clark was convinced many of his young stars would serve the club for years to come. The full squad on the tour consisted of goalkeeper John Broomhead; backs Len Badger, Arthur Armitage, Doug Mountain; half-backs Sam Clarke, Ken Mallender, Roger Hudson, Barry Wagstaffe; forwards Colin Twigg, Michael Ash, John Parkes, Garth Lee, Mick Jones, John Gray, Howard Wilkinson and Tony Wagstaffe.

In 1961/62 Mick continued to develop in the juniors. Sheffield's youngsters won the Northern Intermediate League Cup, 5-1 on aggregate against Sunderland. The victory was a sensational triumph considering five of Sunderland's players had played first team football.

We played in the Northern Intermediate League against some strong teams including Newcastle United and Leeds United (who included the likes of Norman Hunter, Paul Reaney, Gary Sprake, Terry Cooper, Peter Lorimer, Jimmy Greenhoff and Eddie Gray in their side). It was the best standard of football for under-19s in the country, so to win the cup was a great achievement. Once again we went back to Gronigen at the end of the season, although we didn't win the tournament it was great experience.

On 16 November 1962, aged seventeen, Mick Jones signed his first professional contract as a footballer. The *Sheffield Star* reported: 'A player taken on Sheffield United's ground staff after one trial game signed professional forms yesterday. He is Mick Jones, a 17-year-old from Shireoaks, whom manager John Harris describes as having "one of the hardest shots with either foot in the club".'

International tournament in Gronigen, 1962.

On tour with the apprentices, Amsterdam, 1962.

After making headlines in the juniors, Mick made his debut for the reserves at home to Manchester City reserves on Boxing Day 1962. The *Sheffield Star* commented: 'Mick Jones made a dream debut in Sheffield United's Central League line-up, his brilliant performance earning this praise from the club's Football Committee chairman, Dick Wragg: "It is early to forecast, but I think we have an international in the making." Jones was arch schemer of an attack that, in skating rink conditions, was always on top.'

Wragg's prediction would eventually come true, but first there was the small matter of breaking into the first team, a graduation that was soon achieved. Towards the end of the 1962/63 season, Harris began to introduce a number of his promising youngsters to the First XI. Harris believed in a strong youth policy and was committed to developing young players, which promoted loyalty and team spirit. Mick Jones was one of the first to be given his opportunity.

I remember going to the billboard in the dressing room on the Friday afternoon to look at the teamsheet for Saturday's games and expected as usual to be in the reserve team. When I saw my name in the first team to face Manchester United at Old Trafford, I was stunned. In fact I was shaking life a leaf! I went to the team meeting and could not believe that I was sitting with players who were my heroes, in less than twenty-four hours we'd be team-mates. I raced home to tell my parents; I didn't sleep well that night!

On the morning of the match, 20 April 1963, the local press was full of the story. 'A lad who dreamed of wearing the blue and white of Sheffield Wednesday steps out for his League debut today – in the red and white of Sheffield United. He is 17 year old inside forward Mick Jones, tossed into the turbulent waters of the relegation zone against rich, but ragged Manchester United at Old Trafford. Jones, 5ft 10in, who was snapped up from a local colliery side two years ago, gets his chance because regular inside left Billy Hodgson has a groin injury.'

Sheffield United squad, 1962/63.

'Jones rise is phenomenal even by current standards. He started the season with the Northern Intermediate League side and scored 23 goals in 20 games. Moving into the Central League championship-challenging reserve team he got 9 goals in his first 8 matches. Now he steps into the big time. Jones only turned professional last November, his debut is an early birthday gift for he will be 18 next Wednesday.'

Commenting at the time Mick said:

Obviously I'm excited and a little nervous, but I've got my biggest pal, Tony Wagstaffe, in the other inside forward position, so I won't feel too much out of things. Although it's a great chance for me to play in the first team I'll still be wondering how the reserves are going on. I know how much the boss Mr Harris would like us to win that Central League title.

Following his performance in a 1-1 draw, journalists were impressed. John Hathaway in the *Daily Telegraph* wrote, 'John Harris was naturally a little apprehensive about how his youngsters would fare in the battle of Old Trafford. Like many other managers he feels there is a right and a wrong time to thrust teenagers into league football, no matter how hard hit a club are for experienced men. He feels that what happens on the debut day can make or mar a boy's career. However, after seeing the way 17-year old Mick Jones rose to the occasion, I don't think Harris will have any worries about the

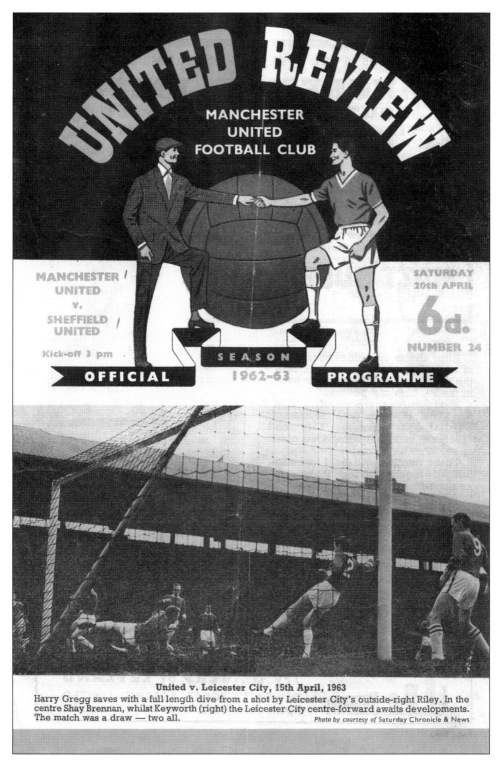

United v. Leicester City, 15th April, 1963

Harry Gregg saves with a full length dive from a shot by Leicester City's outside-right Riley. In the centre Shay Brennan, whilst Keyworth (right) the Leicester City centre-forward awaits developments. The match was a draw — two all.   Photo by courtesy of Saturday Chronicle & News

The programme from the match in which Mick made his Football League debut.

Worksop boy's ability to take it. Jones went through the mill of a typical Manchester repertoire and was certainly bounced around on one or two occasions, but he seemed to revel in it and although he never pulled up any large trees it was certainly a useful debut. In fact, he came within a whisker of celebrating his first appearance with a goal that would have had "gem" written all over it.'

Mick received numerous telegrams following his debut, including one from the Mayor of Worksop, Councillor H.B. Dunn J.P. A few days later Sheffield travelled back across the Pennines to face Manchester City at Maine Road. Mick kept his place in the side and won more plaudits with a sensational display.

Peter Howard, *Sheffield Star*: 'No wonder Sheffield United were all smiles last night. One very good reason for that top-of-the-world feeling in gloomy Manchester weather was a morale-boosting performance from Mick Jones, celebrating his eighteenth birthday in fine style. It was only his second First Division outing, but he played with all the assurance of 102 league matches behind him and scored twice in a 3-1 victory... Jones took his chances in heart-warming style, but this was only the icing on very solid fare provided by the well-built youngster who moves quickly, thinks smartly and is a glutton for work.'

Praise indeed, and it was a time that brings back fond memories:

Everything had happened so quickly for me from joining the ground staff at fifteen. Suddenly I was making my first-team debut against the likes of Bobby Charlton, Denis Law, Bill Foulkes, Paddy Crerand and Nobby Stiles. We drew at Old Trafford and I didn't do too badly, in fact I nearly grabbed the winner with an overhead kick. We really deserved to win that day because we put in a terrific display; the match flew by. Having been used to playing in front of small crowds the noise was deafening. I soon got used to it though. The following Wednesday, we played Manchester City, it was a really rainy night and I scored twice in our 3-1 win – some eighteenth birthday present!

To cap a phenomenal week, Mick made his home debut against Leyton Orient. Lining up alongside him was Tony Wagstaffe (18) and two more promising apprentices making their League debuts, Len Badger (17) and Bernard Shaw (18), as Harris continued his bold policy of blooding his talented youngsters.

As one paper headlined: 'The Young Ones Have Arrived'. The reporter was clearly impressed by Harris's philosophy. 'Sheffield United gave supporters something to talk about and look forward to in the future. Their young players turned in a tremendous performance, and had a major part in this success. The crowd gave them a standing ovation at the end. Supporters will talk about the goal scored by Mick Jones in the twenty-second minute for a long time; a superb header that had Pinner hopelessly beaten.'

Sheffield's manager John Harris was thrilled. 'When these lads were in the 'A' team earlier this season I knew they were all of Division One calibre. They have now proved it by playing together.' Local reporter Peter Howard *Sheffield Star* summed up a tumultuous week for Mick. 'If the whole town is talking about the quiet, unassuming Jones boy of Bramall Lane… I don't blame them. After his remarkable scoring feats for the juniors, many people, me included, were looking forward to the day when "Big Mick" stepped up for first team duty. That day came last Saturday… He came through with flying colours.'

Before the end of the season Sheffield played Tottenham Hotspur, the outstanding team of the early 1960s, who were about to become the first British team to win a European trophy.

I kept my place for the last few games of the season. One match I remember was at Tottenham, who had won the double a couple of years earlier. They were a wonderful team and had the likes of Dave Mackay, Jimmy Greaves, Bobby Smith, John White, Cliff Jones and, of course, Danny Blanchflower, their skipper, still in their side. They won 4-2. I happened to get a goal, so I was quite happy.

Four goals in his six games had local papers eulogising about Sheffield's new striker, and such was his impact that the general consensus among journalists was that he would play for England's under-23 side within a season. Mick, however, wasn't thinking that far ahead, he was just glad to have made the breakthrough into first team football.

Our skipper Cec Coldwell and the other established players were brilliant and helped me settle into the team. As for the manager, John Harris, I owe him so much for having the courage to give me my break in the first team at such a young age. It was obviously a gamble, but he believed in the youth policy at the club and set me on my way far earlier than I could have expected at another club.

Archie Clark and John Short were also great influences during my early years as a player. I had talent, but they developed other areas of my game. On many afternoons they would spend hours with me working to improve my skills.

Believe me you served your apprenticeship, but it paid off because a lot of youngsters made it into the first team. Looking back, the coaches were testing your character, which you needed if you were to make it in professional football. Many lads dropped out, which didn't necessarily mean they weren't good footballers, they just didn't have that something extra to make it as a professional.

Even though I had made my first-team debut I was still able to play for the juniors and helped them win the Northern Intermediate League. After the season had ended I went on the close season tour to Gronigen in Holland. Although the last part of the season had been unbelievable for me, I knew a lot of hard work was ahead.

3
BATTLING BLADE
1963-65

Having made his mark, Mick got the positional move he desired when Harris played him at centre forward against Chelsea in December 1963. His performance in Sheffield's 3-2 defeat won rave reviews. One national paper commented: 'Young Jones was the most impressive youngster of them all, his dash and opportunism gave Chelsea's experienced centre half John Mortimer an edgy ninety minutes'.

A few days later Mick inspired the comeback of the season at Nottingham Forest. Ross Jenkinson of the *Sheffield Telegraph* wrote of the game: 'Incredible... There is no other word to describe it. In 17 minutes you wouldn't have given the stripped bones for United's chances at the City Ground. They were like the babes in the pantomime wood

Sheffield United squad, 1963/64.

Left: Gently does it! Mick scores against Chelsea. Right: A hum-dinger of a match! Forest 3 United 3.

lost, ragged and despondent. Three goals down, and showing no signs of even getting into the match, they tottered their way to half time, no doubt thankful that Forest's early fire had not continued to burn so fiercely.'

The second half was very different and Jenkinson was clearly impressed. 'Two goals by young Mick Jones, the ever-dashing leader who made the seasoned McKinley the most hard-worked man in the match, were further proof that United have saved a lot of cash... Jones produced all that a successful leader needs, above all persistency and enthusiasm. After 60 minutes Jones raced in to volley the ball through as it came over from the right... Normal time had expired when Ash cleverly beat McKinley with a reverse pass that gave Jones a clear path to goal. The youngster took the ball on, and as Grummitt dashed out, hit a left-footer into the net.' Forest clung on in injury time to deny a story that would have gone down as the best of 1963.

On 25 January 1964, Mick penned an article 'Help all the way...' summing up his meteoric rise to fame. His modesty would stay with him throughout his career.

There are times when I'm tempted to give myself a real pinch, to see if I'm awake! A few weeks ago I lived for only an occasional match as stand in with United, never

27

daring to think that fate in the form of an injury to Keith Kettleborough would put me in line for a regular place. That's the way things have turned out, and while I'm sorry it has had to happen like that, please forgive me when I say that I'm also pleased!

Football can be a bitter business, full of jealousies and ill will. I'm lucky; I have not had to bear anything like that, in fact just the opposite. From the first time I came into the first team this season, I have had nothing but help and encouragement from the other players and training staff. The experienced players don't wet-nurse youngsters believe me. They goad and drive them unmercilessly, but behind the scolding and cussing I've had from United men, I know there has always been a reason far removed from jealousy. I've learned quickly how to take criticism from my experienced pals. Not that I don't argue with them!

The early months of 1964 saw Sheffield struggle for goals, but Mick's endeavour was being noted. Following a fine 0-0 draw with defending champions Everton at Bramall Lane, the *Sheffield Telegraph* commented: 'Teenager Jones was the best forward,

Left: FA Cup debut… a brace in a 4-0 canter. Right: 'Derby' debut. A day of woe as United lost 3-0.

Mick in action against Fulham.

brimful of his old early season confidence… He has gunpowder in his boots, and one of these days somebody is going to suffer from the explosion.'

In the latter stages of the season the players rediscovered the form that had seen them briefly lead the table earlier in the campaign. Burnley, Arsenal, Wolves and Fulham were beaten in a six-match spell. The highlight was the clash at home to Wolves, which the Blades won 4-3 in a pulsating encounter. Prior to the match with Burnley, a Sheffield United XI played a friendly with England, a game refereed by Sir Alf Ramsey. England's manager could not have failed to be impressed by Mick's performance: especially his two cracking goals in his side's 3-2 win. The England XI had some notable players in their line-up: Waiters, Cohen, Thompson, Milne, Swan, Flowers, Paine, Eastham, Armfield, Kay, Dobson.

A new team was beginning to take shape, as a number of Harris's young stars cemented their places in the first team. Sheffield ended the season in mid-table. Mick Jones was receiving great press but still had to find his true position, a subject that was creating some debate in the *Sheffield Telegraph*. Benny Hill wrote on 17 April 1964: 'There are different schools of thought on whether Jones plays the more effective role at centre forward, as against inside. What is certain is that quite a number of the top clubs managers are beginning to note the potential in the eighteen-year-old from Worksop. There have, in fact, been whispers in the past few months that here is a young man who could well develop into England material… Physically he is ideally built to take on the bustling, punchy role. He is good with his head and there is thunder in his boots.'

As the future beckoned Mick was still young enough to play for the juniors, indeed whilst playing for the first team he helped the juniors win both the Northern Intermediate League and League Cup for a second time. The cup competition saw Sheffield defeat a particularly strong Leeds United side 3-1 on aggregate.

Mick and another future legend, Len Badger.

The class of 1964.

Sheffield United's youngsters after their cup triumph over Leeds United.

During the close season no one at Bramall Lane could possibly have predicted what the 1964/65 campaign would bring for the young striker. An injury in only the third game of the season to Derek Pace resulted in Mick moving to centre forward, he would make the position his own during the campaign. Making an immediate impact, Mick scored six goals in seven League games. With Pace out, Harris continued his policy of introducing youngsters to the team by giving a debut to Alan Birchenall, who made a spectacular impression by striking eight goals in his opening nine games for the club. Suddenly, Sheffield had a strike-force that appeared to be one of the most exciting around.

Following a 2-1 victory at Fulham, who included Johnny Haynes, George Graham and the mercurial Rodney Marsh in their side, the *Sheffield Telegraph* headlined 'United's Blond Bombers Hit the Jackpot'. The local paper was delighted with the new strike-force: 'Mick Jones and Alan Birchenall, Sheffield United's two young blond bombers, showed just how they could become the First Division's scoring sensations this season when they combined to sink Fulham in devastating style at Craven Cottage last night.'

A few days later Birmingham was dispatched 3-1. 'Blond Bombers Pack a KO Punch' roared the *Sheffield Star*. 'Beware the "blond bombers", the power-packed teenage twins who have taken United soaring to second place in the table today. Alan Birchenall

Sheffield United squad, 1964/65.

Left: Mick battles for possession with West Brom's Stan Jones. Right: The 'blond bombers' in action, Alan Birchenall and Mick Jones.

and Mick Jones are the names defenders should fear… both nineteen, both fair-haired, both ready to swoop like vultures on the half chance that wins matches. They have now scored 11 of United's 12 goals this season, and while they are so menacing United will head right to the top.'

Although understandably exuberant, the *Sheffield Star* was being a little premature; the next victory would follow five defeats in a six-match spell – but what a win, 4-0 at home to Arsenal. Local reporters were delighted, 'Teenage scoring terrors Jones and Birchenall ripped the heart out of hapless Arsenal in chalking up United's best victory of the season.'

By now it was recognised that the campaign would be a steep learning curve for Harris's young side. Another future star, Alan Woodward, had made his debut and impressed, but with so many changes to the team, results suffered, especially after the New Year when only three League fixtures were won.

Apart from cementing his place in Sheffield's team, Mick's club form had won him international recognition when he was called up to England's under-23 squad for a clash with Romania in November 1964. It had been a sensational rise for Mick, who had only been playing first team football for eighteen months.

Cartoon capers.

Mick scores against Everton, but the goal was disallowed.

Mick heads home against West Ham in a 3-1 win.

When Archie Clark told me I was wanted by the boss, and kept his face straight, I thought I was in trouble at first. Then when the manager told me the news, I found it hard to believe because the only representative football I'd played was for Nottinghamshire Schoolboys.

John Harris was thrilled for his young star, 'Jones' selection is no less than he deserves, and this could just be the beginning, especially if Mick continues to develop as he has in the last twelve months.'

England Under-23 v Rumania Under-23: Glazier (Coventry City), Badger (Sheffield United), Thomson (Wolves), Newton (Nottingham Forest), Mobley (Sheffield Wed) captain, Hunter (Leeds United), Murray (Chelsea), Tambling (Chelsea), Jones (Sheffield United), Ball (Blackpool), Hinton (Nottingham Forest).

The actual match could not have gone better for England's under-23 side, and their budding centre forward, who marked his international debut with the opening goal of the match, which set his team on the way to a 5-0 win, all the goals coming in the second half. His goal had unlocked a tight defence – a fact not lost on team manager Sir Alf Ramsey, who thought his opening goal 'destroyed the Romanians'.

The *Sheffield Star* headlined 'Jones-Badger link starts goal rush', and the paper was quick to point out the local perspective. 'When Sheffield United – yes, Sheffield United

– started the rush that brought five goals, the Rumanians crumbled, lost temper and resorted to all manner of obstructions, but in the end were thoroughly thrashed like a pack of naughty boys. The goal rush began when Len Badger planted a long diagonal pass into the middle after holding the ball just long enough for team-mate Mick Jones to take up position. Out came Hajdu; up went Jones, and England were ahead after 57 minutes. It was a perfect club link set to international pattern. To mark his first international with the first goal and a fine victory was a creditable performance by young Jones, and all through he showed that he was by no means above his station in such company.'

I really enjoyed my international debut. Playing for England, initially you tend to find that you play as individuals because it takes time to strike up a relationship in only one or two training sessions. However, there's nothing like pulling on that white shirt with the three lions and representing your country.

In January 1965 an article appeared in Saturday's *Green 'Un* summarising Mick Jones progress, strengths and contribution to the team. 'At one time Jones looked as if he was rather surprised to find himself in first team company, but all this has been left behind in 1964. His strength and speed have always been evident, especially since he started hammering goals with amazing regularity for the juniors. His reading of a game has improved immeasurably, along with his ball control and ability to finish and begin attacks. He has probably had the most difficult task of all the United youngsters,

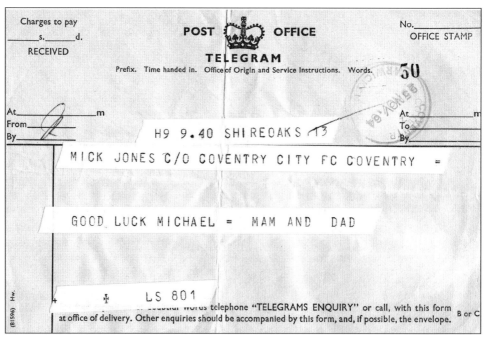

Good luck, son!

From Dinnington to international star in eighteen months.

because centre forward is surely the most trying position in British football at the moment. The coming year should see him hit many more high spots for both club and country.'

Within a month, Mick made his second appearance for the under-23s against Scotland, captained by Billy Bremner. The match ended 0-0, but Jones had further enhanced his growing reputation.

Scotland Under-23 v England Under-23: Glazier (Coventry City), Badger (Sheffield United), Reaney (Leeds United), Stiles (Manchester United), Mobley (Sheffield Wed, captain), Hunter (Leeds United), Murray (Chelsea), Chivers (Southampton), Jones (Sheffield United), Ball (Blackpool), Sissons (West Ham).

"UNDER 23's"
INTERNATIONAL

ENGLAND

VERSUS

RUMANIA

Wednesday, 25th November, 1964
Kick-off 7.30 p.m.

*Official Programme
for the first International match to be played
on the Highfield Road Stadium*

PRICE SIXPENCE

Against Scotland, Billy Bremner and Alan Ball had a right go at each throughout the match, you could tell they'd be great players. We drew 0-0, it was a really tough game, but very enjoyable.

Following a third cap for England's Under-23 side in a 0-0 draw against Czechoslovakia, Mick made an appearance for Young England in their 2-2 draw against England.

United ended the season in nineteenth place, which was quite misleading because only one point was gained from the last eight matches. However, the future looked exciting with the promotion of so many youngsters to the side. The Jones-Birchenall partnership had been the high point, when their goals, especially during the early stages of the season had proved crucial. It was Mick though who took the individual scoring honours, finishing the League campaign as top scorer for the first time with 14 goals.

I was delighted how the season had gone because I'd held my own against the likes of Ron Yeats, Dave Mackay, Frank McLintock, Bill Foulkes, Brian Labone and Norman Hunter. My partnership with Alan Birchanell had also developed. He joined as an apprentice a year after me and quickly made an impression. Scoring a lot of goals

Len Badger and Mick bound for Scotland with England's under 23 squad.

A clash with the Jocks.

Checkmate!

ENGLAND v. YOUNG ENGLAND

Team Manager: A. E. Ramsey

Team Physician: Dr. A. L. Bass

ENGLAND TEAM

(White shirts, dark blue shorts, white stockings):-

Goalkeeper:	G. Banks (Leicester City)
Right Back:	G. Cohen (Fulham)
Left Back:	R. Wilson (Everton)
Right Half Back:	N. P. Stiles (Manchester United)
Centre Half Back:	R. Flowers (Wolverhampton W.)
Left Half Back:	R. Moore (West Ham U.) Captain
Outside Right:	J. Connelly (Manchester United)
Inside Right:	J. Greaves (Tottenham Hotspur)
Centre Forward:	B. Bridges (Chelsea)
Inside Left:	G. Eastham (Arsenal)
Outside Left:	R. Charlton (Manchester United)
Reserve:	D. Temple (Everton)
Trainer:	H. Shepherdson (Middlesbrough)

YOUNG ENGLAND

(Red shirts, red shorts, red stockings):-

Goalkeeper:	G. West (Everton)
Right Back:	L. Badger (Sheffield United)
Left Back:	R. Thomson (Wolves) Captain
Right Half Back:	J. Hollins (Chelsea)
Centre Half Back:	V. J. Mobley (Sheffield W.)
Left Half Back:	M. Peters (West Ham United)
Outside Right:	A. Murray (Chelsea)
Inside Right:	R. Tambling (Chelsea)
Centre Forward:	M. Jones (Sheffield United)
Inside Left:	A. Ball (Blackpool)
Outside Left:	G. Armstrong (Arsenal)
Reserve:	M. H. Chivers (Southampton)
Trainer:	B. Mee (Arsenal)

**ARRANGEMENTS FOR TRAVEL AND
ACCOMMODATION**

———————

Headquarters:

**WINDSOR HOTEL,
LANCASTER GATE,
PADDINGTON, W.2.**

(Telephone: Ambassador 4501)

THURSDAY, 29th APRIL, 1965

ASSEMBLY. Players should make their own travel arrangements in order to arrive at Headquarters by 12.30 p.m. The bus will leave the Windsor Hotel, at 2.00 p.m. for Highbury.

FRIDAY, 30th APRIL, 1965

5.00 p.m.   Tea.

5.30 p.m.   A motor coach will leave for Arsenal Stadium.

7.30 p.m.   ENGLAND

v.

YOUNG ENGLAND.

After the match the coach will return to Headquarters.

SATURDAY, 1st MAY, 1965

Arrangements will be made for those players who so wish to attend the Cup Final.

Spotting talent for the forthcoming World Cup.

Left: Some of England's finest youngsters. From left to right: Nobby Stiles, Bobby Tambling, Bobby Thomson, Alan Ball and Mick Jones. Right: Catching a lift from the great Joe Shaw.

JOE SHAW
TESTIMONIAL FUND

**Sheffield United
v Selected XI**

Monday, 29th March, 1965

Kick-off 7.30 p.m.

ROW   SEAT

EE | 7

—Drawn by Heap

BENEFIT MATCH

EAST WING

RESERVED SEAT 9/-

Match ticket for Joe Shaw's testimonial match.

he forced his way into the first team alongside me. We became quite a force in attack, even though we were similar in style. At times we did get in each other's way going for the same ball, but we settled down and caused defences problems. Birchy was a one off – a real character.

Towards the end of the campaign I played in Joe Shaw's testimonial match. This game was special because Joe, who had taken over from Cec Coldwell as skipper, had been a big influence on my early career. The apprentices called him 'Dad': he was a super professional. The All-Star XI that night had some wonderful players, including the great Sir Stanley Matthews. This showed the esteem Joe was held in. Playing for Sheffield was Jimmy Hagan, acknowledged as the greatest Sheffield United player ever. Jimmy was meant to play for the All-Star XI, but agreed to play for us, which delighted everyone. Before the game he asked me who I was. I said 'Jones, Mr Hagan'. He said, 'Listen Jones, when you get out on that pitch, I don't want the ball five yards left, five yards right or five yards in front of me, I want it to the feet. Do you understand? I said 'Right Mr Hagan'.

It was a full house and I was determined to impress. I passed the ball five yards in front of Jimmy… he gave me a glare and wagged a finger at me to come over to him. He was not impressed! It was a wonderful occasion even though we lost 6-5 after leading 5-1. Jimmy Greaves scored a hat-trick for the All-Stars. I was satisfied though

Mick's call-up schedule for England's post-season tour.

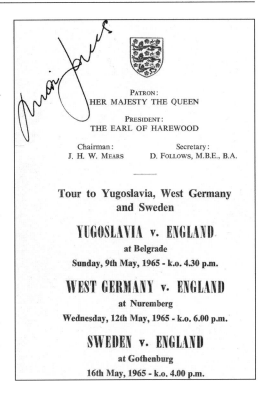

because both Jimmy Hagan and myself scored. Jimmy may have retired, but he could still play a bit. Afterwards he asked me who I was again, so I told him. He said, 'Now look Jones, you may have a bit of a chance in this game if you keep at it'. Coming from the great man meant a lot to me. It had been a great night, especially for Joe Shaw.

At the end of the season there would be one final surprise – a call-up to the full England squad for their summer tour to Yugoslavia, West Germany and Sweden. With England's manager still evaluating players for the World Cup

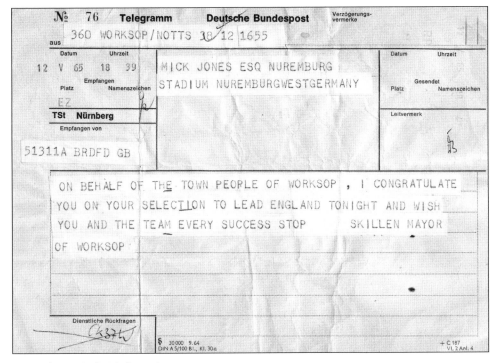

Best wishes to Worksop's favourite son.

finals, his elevation to the full squad was sensational news. Could Mick make the final squad? Unthinkable at the start of the season, suddenly it was a possibility.

Ramsey's biggest headache at the time was the centre forward position. Likened to Tottenham ace Bobby Smith, Mick was seen as a possibility to team up with the great Jimmy Greaves. His inclusion was certainly seen as a gamble, with the likes of Joe Baker, Alan Peacock, Alan Wignall and Fred Pickering cold-shouldered. (At this stage another young player, Geoff Hurst, had not been a part of the full England set-up yet!)

I was stunned! I hadn't thought for one moment I'd be chosen. When I saw the letter lying on the dressing room table, I thought it might be an invitation to the under-23 tour.

Following a 1-1 draw against Yugoslavia, Ramsey made a number of changes in midfield and attack. His defence though was the one area that was becoming settled and would remain unchanged throughout the World Cup. Mick made his full England debut against West Germany in Nuremburg.

Being on tour was a tremendous experience. Alf was fantastic: he made me feel really at ease. He was extremely knowledgeable and never got flustered. He simply asked

you to do what you did at club level. The night before the West Germany game we went down to the stadium to train on the pitch. During the session I was on my own in one of the goal areas when Alf came over and told me I was playing. I was stunned and didn't know what to say.

West Germany v England: Banks (Leicester City), Cohen (Fulham), Wilson (Everton), Flowers (Wolves), Charlton (Leeds United), Moore (West Ham, captain), Paine (Southampton), Ball (Blackpool), Jones (Sheffield United), Eastham (Arsenal), Temple (Everton).

In a superb display, England recorded the third of a post-war hat-trick of victories over West Germany.

What a baptism – West Germany.

Sir Alf's boys of 1965. Mick is pictured second from right.

Presentation av ENGLANDS spelare

★ **GORDON BANKS**, Leicester. — Köptes för en struntsumma från Chesterfield 1959 och har sen dess spelat bl a 2 cupfinaler (1961-1963), ingendera vunnen... Har vaktat Englands mål 15 gånger. I fjol ville han flytta men Leicester satte ett sånt pris (750.000 kr) på honom, att ingen klubb hade råd att reflektera. Bergsäker på höjdbollar, men markbollar kan möjligen slinka in.

★ **TONY WAITERS**, Blackpool. — Har vikarierat et par gånger i A-landslaget när UK ansett att Banks borde vila sig ett slag. Stor bjässe som bl a vaktade Englands mål i Sir Stanleys avskedsmatch häromveckan. På samrarna ägnar han sig ät sitt jobb nr 2 – livräddare.

★ **GEORG COHEN**, Fulham. — Erövrade ordinarie backplats i fjol under amerikaturnén och har hittils gjort 15 A-kamper. Tottenham bjöd 80.000 pund (1,4 milj) på men Fulham nobbade!

★ **RAY WILSON**, Everton. — Blev ordinarie back redan som div II-spelare i Hudderfield. Nu åter tillbaka efter knäskada. Everton betalade i somras 30.000 pund för robuste Ray. Den transfersumman (450.000 kr) skulle Hudds spelare få dela på, ifall dom klarade uppflyttning från div II — det gick nu inte. Har bl a kämpat väl mot Garrincha i VM 1962. Sedan 1960 har han erövrat 31 caps d v s den mössa som följer varje landskampsuppdrag.

★ **KEITH NEWTON**, Blackburn. — Flera ungdomslandskamper men ingen ännu i A-laget. Newton (23) spelar lika bra på båda backplatserna.

★ **NOBBY STILES**, Manchester U. — Ettrig tuffing (23) som bidragit till att "Busy Babes" vann ligamästerskapet. Är egentligen defensiv 4–2–4 halvback men fick debutera mot Skottland för nån månad sen som förbindelselänk på mittfältet.

★ **JACKIE CHARLTON**, Leeds. — Först i vår erkänd som storspelare och debuterade mot Skottland. Nu Englands ordinarie stopper. Leeds och sedan 1952 och ända tills i år omnämnd bara som mer berömde "Bobby Charltons bror". Trots sin broders stadgade rykte som mindre farlig herre har faktiskt storebror Jackie (28) förutom försvarssysslo hunnit med att göra 10 mål på fri sparkar och innickade hörnar! D v s tre ggr så många som Bobby! En lång räkel med stor räckvidd och bombsäkert huvudspel.

★ **BOBBY MOORE**, West Ham. — Har varit kapten för alla lag han spelat i! 18 ggr i Englands U-landslag, 9 ggr i landslaget för Under 23-åringar och 27 A-landskamper före denna kontinentturne. Valdes i fjol till Årets Spelare och ledde West Ham till cupfinalvinst (över Preston). Stor domnerande, majestätisk blond bjässe med mestadels defensiv huvuduppgift. Englands 4–2–4-system har en av sina stötespelare i "Hammarnas" kapten, given i VM nästa år.

★ **RON FLOWERS**, Wolverhampton. — Legendariska "Vargarna" har varit i rejält blåsväder hela säsongen och också åkt ur div II. Men en som hela tiden kämpat med näbbar och klor är Varga-kaporen Flowers. "Den blonde tigern har i sista stund kallats 'under fanorna'. Den årrige "batalijhästen" är rutinerad värre. 45 landskamper har han gjort, dock ingen det sista året.

★ **TERRY PAINE**, Southampton. — Blev proffs 1957 och har trots div II adressen ett 10-tal A-landskamper. Mycket snabb och svårfångad ytter, vilken storklubbarna, särskilt Tottenham, länge haft ett gott öga till.

★ **PETER THOMPSON**, Liverpool. — Vy i klubb- men hy i landslaget 11 gånger. Kom ursprungligen från Preston och debuterade i A-landslaget i fjol då han deltog i sydamerikaturnen och s k Lilla VM, där

dock Englands framgångar inte var särskilt lysande. God dribblare och snabb, passningssäker herre, men inte sverdeles målfarlig. Kostade "Beatlepool" 600.000 kr i aug 1963 och har sen dess hjälpt dom "Röda Djävlarna" att vinna ligamästerskapet 1964, cupfinalen 1965 och är nu i Europacupfinalen.

★ **JIMMY GREAVES**, Tottenham. — Har blivit engelska ligans skyttekung tre år i rad. Har gjort över 200 liga- och cupmål vid bara 25 års ålder. Landslagets främste målspottare med 38 mål på 44 matcher! Spelade något år i Milan, trivdes inte och återköptes 1961 för 99.999 pund (1,5 milj kr) men inte av sin gamla klubb Chelsea utan av Tottenham. Inte precis kanonskytt, men rinner som en oljad blixt genom försvaren och gör mål på "kvartschanser". Allra farligast är hans vänsterfot! Se opp!

★ **BARRY BRIDGES**, Chelsea. — Spelade redan i fjol på Ullevi i Chelseas strålande uppvisning mot

Kamraterna. En av Englands snabbaste centerforwards och sin klubbs ledande målskytt (25 fullträffar i år). 24-årige Barry är gift med en polska och äger tillsammans med svärfar ett 27-rums hotell i Eastbourne. Vilket betyder att han 5 dar i veckan för kuska 20 svenska mil för träning och matcher på hemmaplanen Stamford Bridge i London. 2 landskamper. Hittils.

★ **BOBBY CHARLTON**, Manchester U. — Englands meste landskampare med 57 "kepsar". Då han och broderskapet Jackie spelade mot Skottland vid det första tillfället gången att brödrapar burit Englands vita blusar detta århundrade. Agare till en jätteharlig vänsterfot!

★ **GEORGE EASTHAM**, Arsenal. — Sen 1963 har denne arsenolstrateg gjort 13 A-landskamper. Vad som ligger den rätt snobbe innern i fatet är att han just kommer bort i ro busta närkamper. Han undviker sådana och för han vara i relativt "fred" är han ypperlig spelförde lare och målskytt.

★ **JOHN CONNELLY**, Manchester U. — Snabb och rakt-på-mål-rusande ytter. Landslagsspelare 10 gånger i A-laget under sin Burnley-tid bl a mot Sverige, som då vann med 3–2 på Wembley.

★ **ALAN BALL**, Blackpool. — En av påläggskalvarna inom engelsk fotboll och ett av de största innerlöftena. Redan bofast i landslaget för Under 23-åringar. Rödhårige Alan har dock ett så ilsket temperament — som går ut över bl a domarna — att han blev diskad 14 dar i januari.

★ **DEREK TEMPLE**, Everton. — Mattnytig, talangfull ytter som Alf Ramsey, Englands manager, ställer vissa förhoppningar på inför VM nästa år.

★ **MIKE JONES**, Sheffield U. — Centerproblemet är inte löst ännu. Sen bjässen Bobby Smith slutade har dar i veckan för kuska och nå byrta efter den rötte kedjeledaren. Även den kraftige Jones ska få sin chans.

6   7

England player profiles for the clash with Sweden.

ITINERARY

———

**ARRANGEMENTS FOR TRAVEL
AND ACCOMMODATION**

SUNDAY, 23rd MAY, 1965

ASSEMBLY. Players must make their own arrangements to assemble at the Windsor Hotel, Lancaster Gate, London, W.2 during the evening where accommodation has been reserved.

MONDAY, 24th MAY, 1965

07.00 hrs. A motor coach will leave the Hotel for London Airport.
08.40 hrs. Depart London Airport (Central) (Flight SR 115).
11.00 hrs. Arrive Basle Airport.
A motor coach will meet the party and convey them to the Hotel Colombi, Freiberg or Luisenhoehe Hotel, Horben.

TUESDAY, 25th MAY, 1965

18.15 hrs. GERMANY v. ENGLAND (at the Moesle Stadium).
21.30 hrs. The Football Association officials and players will be the guests of the German Football Association at Dinner.

WEDNESDAY, 26th MAY, 1965

Arrangements for the day will be announced at Headquarters.

THURSDAY, 27th MAY, 1965

11.30 hrs. Depart Basle Airport (Flight SR.115).
12.00 hrs. Arrive Zurich Airport.
Luncheon at Airport.
13.55 hrs. Depart Zurich (Flight OK 546).

15.05 hrs. Arrive PRAGUE.
Transport will be available to convey the party to the Slaty Lav Hotel, Liberec.

FRIDAY, 28th MAY, 1965

The programme will be announced at Headquarters.

SATURDAY, 29th MAY, 1965

CZECHOSLOVAKIA v. ENGLAND.
After the match the officials and players will be the guests of the Czechoslovak Football Association at dinner.

SUNDAY, 30th MAY, and MONDAY, 31st MAY, 1965

The programme will be announced at the Headquarters.

TUESDAY, 1st JUNE, 1965

12.00 hrs. Depart Prague. (Charter Flight.)
13.10 hrs. Arrive Vienna.
Party will be met and transport provided to the Park Hotel, Schönbrunn, Vienna.

WEDNESDAY, 2nd JUNE, 1965

17.30 hrs. AUSTRIA v. ENGLAND (at the Vienna Stadium).
After the match the officials and players will be the guests of the Austrian Football Association at Dinner.

THURSDAY, 3rd JUNE, 1965

13.45 hrs. Depart Vienna Airport (Flight BA 519).
16.00 hrs. Arrive at London Airport.
A motor coach will meet the party and convey them to The Football Association offices and London Railway Termini.

Not one summer tour but two – England's under-23 itinerary.

The national papers were impressed. 'Jones Shines as England Romp Home!' headlined one. They were fulsome in their praise for the young forward: 'Jones put the team in good spirit right from the start. With almost his first kick Jones had the ball in the net. In the fourth minute he had a shot which brought the best save of the match from Tilkowski. Jones continued to move intelligently and keep the German defence at full stretch. He was unlucky with a header that ran across the face of the goal, though he missed a great chance by heading straight at the 'keeper midway through the second half.'

England's team manager was impressed with his new striker, who was the youngest ever to represent his country. 'I thought Jones came through with flying colours. He is only twenty and this was a tough one to start in. He did remarkably well.'

It was a hard game and the pace never slackened. I was happy overall how my debut had gone and I played a part in our goal by Terry Paine.

His performance earned him a second cap against Sweden. England won this game 2-1. Sweden v England: Banks (Leicester City), Cohen (Fulham), Wilson (Everton), Stiles (Manchester United), Charlton (Leeds United), Moore (West Ham, captain), Paine (Southampton), Ball (Blackpool), Jones (Sheffield United), Eastham (Arsenal), Connelly (Manchester United).

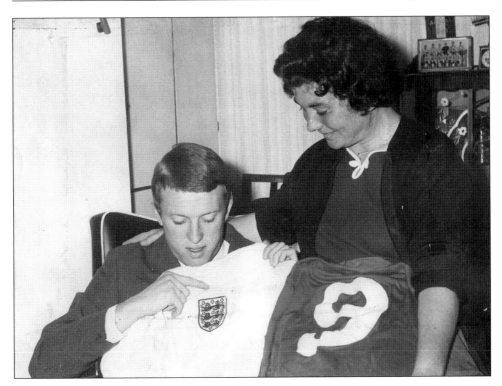

Mick shows his mum a couple of souvenirs from his England travels.

What do you reckon lads?

We won, but the day of the game I didn't feel well and had a poor match. However, to play with Bobby Moore, George Cohen, Ray Wilson, Nobby Stiles, Gordon Banks, Jack Charlton and Alan Ball was a fantastic thrill. A year later they all played in England's 1966 World Cup triumph.

The season was not quite over though, because Mick had also been chosen for the under-23 tour to West Germany, Czechoslovakia and Austria. Gaining more experience in England's 1-0 defeat to West Germany, a tough encounter that was marred by the referee being far too lenient. An injury in a 0-0 draw with Austria brought a memorable campaign to a close.

4
THE SWINGING SIXTIES
1965-67

The early stages of the 1965/66 League campaign followed the pattern of the previous season. By October the Blades were riding high in top spot after a number of impressive victories, the highlight being a rare win at Anfield when Mick scored the crucial goal in the club's first victory at the ground since 1946. Peter Howard in the *Green 'Un* thought the display was the 'finest tactical performance ever from a Sheffield United side away from home… a result that will have shaken a few cynics'.

Sheffield United squad, 1965/66. From left to right, back row: Richardson, Badger, Munks, Matthewson, Hartle. Middle row: Mallender, Jones, Hodgkinson, G. Shaw, J. Shaw. Front row: Birchenall, Docherty, Reece, Coldwell, Wagstaff, Woodward, Kettleborough.

Historic League win at Anfield – the first in two decades.

Left: United hammer the Hammers... Moore, Hurst, Peters and all! Right: Mick's brace wins a thriller against Stoke.

Ten days later, West Ham (a side which included Moore, Hurst and Peters) were defeated 5-3 in a match described as 'the greatest show on earth' by the *Sheffield Telegraph*. According to the *Green 'Un* on Saturday evening, 'the Hammers were bewildered, baffled and really shaken' by an attacking onslaught which had a crowd of 15,796 'roaring their heads off and singing Ilkley Moor Bahtat in a manner usually reserved for cup outings'.

It was an incredible match against West Ham. We were 3-1 up at the interval, but they soon equalised. Fortunately, I managed to get a couple late on to claim a memorable win.

A draw at Blackburn in their eleventh League game of the season saw Sheffield top the table. Victories over Northampton and Stoke City kept them at the summit. However, Mick's form had dipped after a flurry of goals in the opening games. It cost him his place in the full England squad to face Wales.

Naturally I was disappointed because once you played in the First XI you didn't want to give it up. However, I was still young so had time to impress Alf that I could do it for England.

Some consolation came when Mick was picked for an Under-23s clash with France, a match in which he scored twice. The first goal resulted from a mistake by the French 'keeper, the second came late on when he connected with a cross from Martin Chivers to drive the ball home from the edge of the penalty area.

Domestic form suddenly slipped with three consecutive defeats, the last a 6-2 drubbing at Arsenal, which cast doubts on the team's ability to mount a sustained challenge for the title. However, the team responded in the best way possible, with a 2-0 win over Everton, including a brace from their centre forward.

Call-up papers for a clash with France Under 23s.

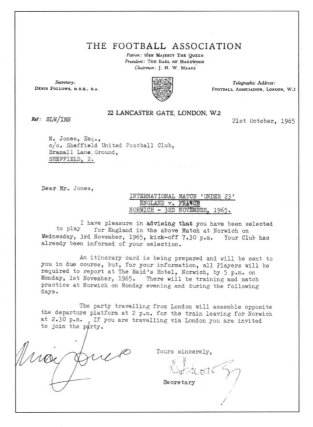

THE FOOTBALL ASSOCIATION

Patron: HER MAJESTY THE QUEEN
President: THE EARL OF HAREWOOD
Chairman: J. H. W. MEARS

Secretary:
DENIS FOLLOWS, M.B.E., B.A.

Telegraphic Address:
FOOTBALL ASSOCIATION, LONDON, W.2

22 LANCASTER GATE, LONDON, W.2

Ref: SLW/IMN

21st October, 1965

M. Jones, Esq.,
c/o. Sheffield United Football Club,
Bramall Lane Ground,
SHEFFIELD, 2.

Dear Mr. Jones,

INTERNATIONAL MATCH 'UNDER 23'
ENGLAND v. FRANCE
NORWICH - 3RD NOVEMBER, 1965.

I have pleasure in advising that you have been selected to play for England in the above Match at Norwich on Wednesday, 3rd November, 1965, kick-off 7.30 p.m. Your Club has already been informed of your selection.

An itinerary card is being prepared and will be sent to you in due course, but, for your information, all Players will be required to report at The Maid's Hotel, Norwich, by 5 p.m. on Monday, 1st November, 1965. There will be training amd match practice at Norwich on Monday evening and during the following days.

The party travelling from London will assemble opposite the departure platform at 2 p.m. for the train leaving for Norwich at 2.30 p.m. If you are travelling via London you are invited to join the party.

Yours sincerely,

Secretary

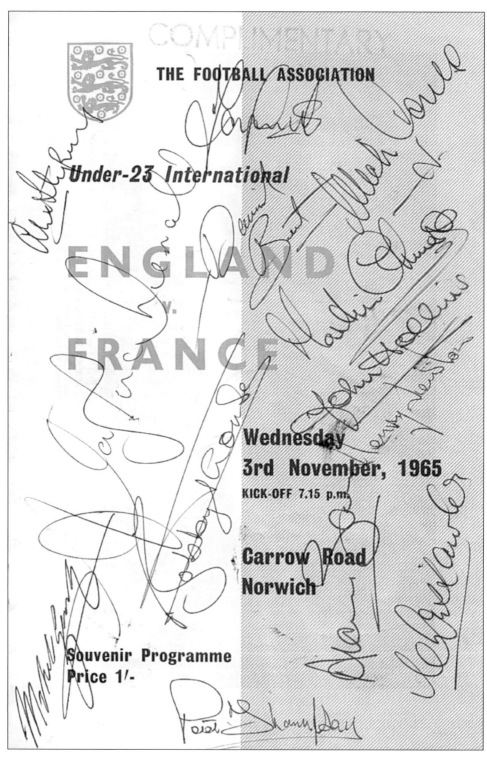

Star autographs.

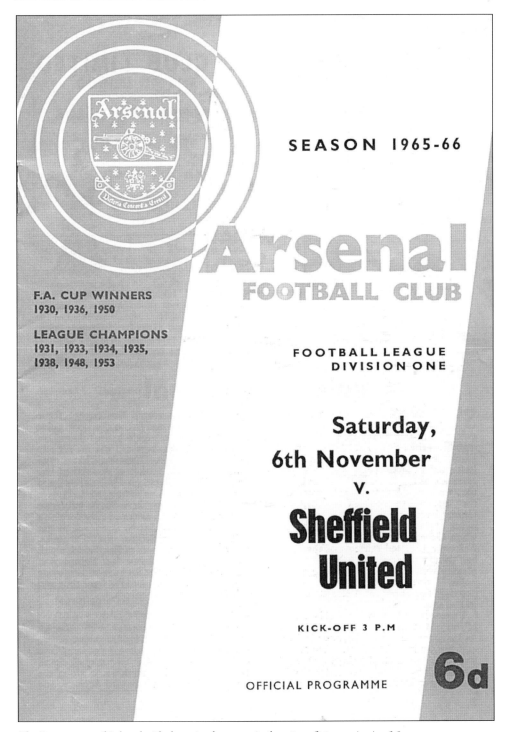

SEASON 1965-66

F.A. CUP WINNERS
1930, 1936, 1950

LEAGUE CHAMPIONS
1931, 1933, 1934, 1935,
1938, 1948, 1953

Arsenal
FOOTBALL CLUB

FOOTBALL LEAGUE
DIVISION ONE

Saturday,
6th November
v.

Sheffield
United

KICK-OFF 3 P.M

OFFICIAL PROGRAMME

6d

The Gunners won 6-2, but the Blades gained revenge in the return fixture, winning 3-0.

Hugh Jamieson was delighted. 'The day of reckoning for Mick Jones was long overdue, the sharp-shooting self-styled "sheriff" from Shireoaks knew it and so did United manager John Harris. The big trouble has been the length of time it has taken twenty-year-old Jones to bare his teeth and start clearing a path to goal that his all-round footballing ability is made to measure for. In simple terms, he is too nice a guy, but get his back up, his red hair fairly bristles and he is twice the player. Everton made this mistake. They roughed up Jones from the start and did United a good turn…'

'For Jones, the subject of late tackles galore, made Everton pay for their bullying with two goals that were like rays of sunshine peeping through the murk of a November afternoon. His first was a neat quickstep in a packed goalmouth, which made enough room to score with a low shot through a forest of legs, but when four tackles later he thumped the ground in frustration… the centre forward was an angry young man. He threw what respect he had left for Everton out of the window and set forth on his one-man act of settling score for score, tackle for tackle. In that mood he was able to lift his game… and true to story-book style had the last word with the perfect finish seven minutes from the end.'

Off the field, public relations were important and Mick did his share on behalf of the club. A couple of days before the Everton clash he made a visit to his old school, to show the junior boys and girls his England caps and sign autographs. The local papers were present. Mr Cope, now headmaster, appreciated the visit from his former pupil.

Back to school!

'This is typical of Michael. We are proud of him at Shireoaks where he captained the first school football team that I formed… Michael has retained all the characteristics, which he had as a boy, such as modesty and dedication, and he is a credit to his profession in every way… Children need heroes, and in these days of long hair and doubtful values among so many teenagers, to give them an example of Michael to look up to can do nothing but good. As successful as he has been to date… Michael is always ready to give credit to those who helped him reach the top.'

Mick's return to form resulted in an increase in confidence, so necessary for strikers. He went on to score seven goals in an eight-game spell, a period in which he won his seventh under-23 cap for England in a 2-1 victory over Yugoslavia. After the players had overturned a deficit to win the match, the *Sheffield Telegraph* felt some of the players may have a chance of making a last ditch bid for Alf Ramsey's World Cup squad, 'especially Jones, who scored the first goal with a corkscrew shot and was always in the thick of it'.

England Under-23 v Yugoslavia Under-23: Stepney (Millwall), Lawler (Liverpool), Thomson (Wolves), Hollins (Chelsea), Mobley (Sheffield Wed, captain), Smith (Liverpool), Armstrong (Arsenal), Hunt (Wolves), Jones (Sheffield United), Chivers (Southampton), Rogers (Swindon).

Although there was clearly an improvement in form, an inconsistent spell saw Sheffield drop down the table, despite Mick's efforts. Following a 1-1 draw against Nottingham Forest, there was a stark warning from one reporter: 'Sheffield United are becoming a club of three sections: cricket, football and Mick Jones'. Jones apart, he was not impressed by United's overall performance. 'Jones had to chase and search, wait and hope. If he ever tires of doing it… United will be in trouble.'

He needn't have worried. Whereas the previous campaign had yielded just three League wins after the turn of the year, seven victories this time around would see the team finish ninth. Progress was being made and Harris's young team was getting more experienced.

Mick scored the opener in a fine win.

ENGLISH FOOTBALL ASSOCIATION

INTERNATIONAL
UNDER 23

ENGLAND

versus

YUGOSLAVIA

THE DELL
SOUTHAMPTON

kick off 7.30 p.m.

WEDNESDAY
24th NOVEMBER 1965

PROGRAMME PRICE SIXPENCE

WORLD CUP WILLIE

Merry Christmas everyone!

There were some stirring performances during the second half of the campaign, and none more bruising than an encounter at Elland Road, when Mick's strike earned a 1-1 draw with Leeds United. According to the *Sheffield Telegraph*, after being put clear by Barry Wagstaffe's astute forward pass, 'Jones took his chance superbly, running on and sweeping the ball past Sprake as the goalkeeper moved out'.

I played against Leeds United a number of times when they had a reputation for being a very physical side. Don Revie moulded the team around Bobby Collins, who though hard, was also a great player for the club. Playing against him and the likes of Billy Bremner, John Giles, Norman Hunter and Willie Bell was difficult; I was certainly glad to play most of my career with them and not against them! They did have a reputation in the mid-sixties but got results.

Towards the end of the season Mick passed a couple of landmarks. Firstly when he made his 100th League appearance for the Blades, scoring in a 2-0 win over Blackburn Rovers, before notching his 50th goal in all competitions for the club in a fine 2-0 win at Newcastle United a day before his twenty-first birthday. In between these fixtures, Sheffield played Blackpool and Everton, a team unbeaten in fourteen matches and having conceded no goals in the previous eight games.

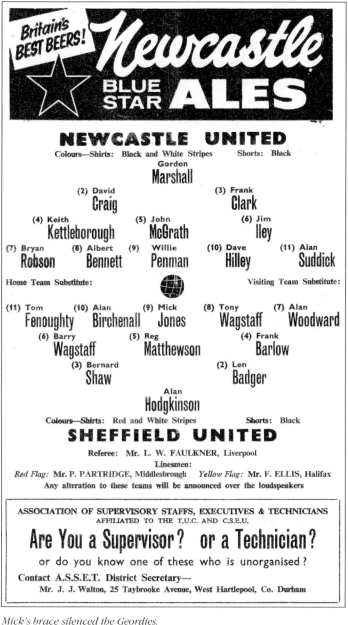

Mick's brace silenced the Geordies.

Following this game, a night on the town resulted in a showdown with the boss.

During Easter, we played at Blackpool and Everton on consecutive days. After a 2-1 defeat to Blackpool we travelled to Southport and stayed overnight. A few of us went out for a walk and saw a bar. We knew it was sacrilege to have a drink before a game, especially with our manager being teetotal, but being young, we thought one shandy would do no harm. As we were getting our drinks, who should walk in but John Harris and two directors.

John whisked the directors off before they saw us, but we knew that we were in trouble. Back at the hotel the manager summoned us. We had the book thrown at us and had a week's wages docked. We beat Everton 3-1, I scored twice, but I was more worried what I'd say to my Mum, because she relied on the £5 a week I gave her out of my wages. When I gave her no money the following week she never said a word, but must have known that I'd got into a scrape. I paid her back the week after.

A few days after the Everton clash, Mick would make another appearance for the under-23s, against Turkey, a match when for the first time three Sheffield United players would represent an England XI. It is interesting to note that there was still

---

SELECTION (Under 23) COMMITTEE:

I. Robinson (Chairman)
S. Bolton
F. A. Davis
S/Ldr. G. A. Hadley
Lt. Col. C. F. Linnitt, J.P., B.Sc.
Lt. Col. G. J. Mitchell, O.B.E.
E. D. Smith
T. V. Williams

MEMBERS OF SELECTION COMMITTEE IN CHARGE:

I. Robinson

ENGLAND TEAM:
(White shirts, dark blue shorts, white stockings).

Goalkeeper:	A. Stepney (Millwall)
Right Back:	R. Badger (Sheffield United)
Left Back:	R. Thomson (Wolves) Captain
Right Half Back:	B. O'Neil (Burnley)
Centre Half Back:	G. Cross (Leicester City)
Left Half Back:	M. Peters (West Ham United)
Outside Right:	M. Summerbee (Manchester City)
Inside Right:	R. Hunt (Wolverhampton W.)
Centre Forward:	M. Jones (Sheffield United)
Inside Left:	A. Birchenall (Sheffield United)
Outside Left:	G. Armstrong (Arsenal)

Reserves to Travel: W. Glazier (Coventry City)
R. Boyce (West Ham United)
F. Saul (Tottenham Hotspur)

Team Manager: A. E. Ramsey

Hon. Team Physician: Dr. U. N. Phillips

Trainer: H. Shepherdson (Middlesbrough)

Headquarters:
THE CLIFTON HOTEL, BLACKPOOL
(Telephone: Blackpool 21481)

ARRANGEMENTS FOR TRAVEL AND ACCOMMODATION

MONDAY, 18th APRIL, 1966

ASSEMBLY. Players should make their own travel arrangements in to order arrive at Manchester City Football Ground, by 3.00 p.m. The party travelling from London will assemble in the main line booking hall at Euston Station by 11.30 a.m. Tickets have been taken and seats reserved on the train leaving at 2.40 p.m. During the afternoon there will be training and match practice on the ground of the Manchester City Football Club. On completion of training a motor coach will leave for Blackpool.

TUESDAY, 19th APRIL, 1966

There will be training at the Blackpool F.C. ground.

WEDNESDAY, 20th APRIL, 1966

5.30 p.m. Motor Coach will depart for Blackburn F.C.

7.24 p.m. Both the English and the Turkish teams must be ready to leave the dressing rooms. The two captains will lead the teams on to the arena, side by side, followed by the referee and linesmen. They will then proceed on either side of the halfway line to the centre of the field. The left column will wheel to the left and the right column to the right. The two teams will then be in line in the centre of the field with the referee and linesmen taking up their positions between the two teams facing the Grand Stand. The National Anthems will then be played after which the teams may "kick about" until the referee calls the captains together to begin the game.

7.30 p.m. ENGLAND v. TURKEY.

After the match the motor coach will proceed to the White Bull Hotel, Blackburn, where players and officials are invited to be the guests of The Football Association at Dinner. After the Dinner those players unable to return to their homes will be taken to the Queens Hotel Manchester where reservations have been made for the night.

THURSDAY, 21st APRIL, 1966 Dispersal.

'Treble' Blades – a historic night for the club.

time for players to impress and win a place in Alf Ramsey's World Cup squad, as Martin Peters, who played that day, clearly did.

I actually got in the last twenty-eight for the '66 World Cup, but missed out on the final squad. I've always been proud of getting so far, but losing out to Geoff Hurst, Jimmy Greaves and Roger Hunt was no disgrace.

Although Mick failed to ultimately make England's squad in 1966, he did finish as the club's top-scorer again in 1965/66, this time with 21 League goals. On a historical note, Mick's goal-scoring exploits in the League would not be bettered until Keith Edwards scored 34 goals in the club's Division Four championship success in 1981/82, and has still to be equalled, let alone beaten, in a top-flight campaign.

At the end of the season, before the players could settle down for the World Cup finals, Mick joined the rest of the squad on a six-week post-season tour.

After a couple of games in Norway, we flew to Mexico. My first game of the trip was in Mexico City twenty-four hours after we arrived, without any acclimatisation at all.

I'd never experienced conditions like it. The altitude and humidity made life extremely difficult, especially kicking off at midday. In our dressing room were two oxygen tanks. After about fifteen minutes, I could barely catch my breath, and collapsed. Next thing I knew I was back in the dressing room taking, in oxygen. I was confined to bed for a few days.

We played in some real dives, especially in Paraguay when the organisers had to get rid of six cows, and cow pats, before we could begin the game! Fortunately, that was the final game of the tour. I was glad to get home for the World Cup, where I saw Portugal play Brazil during the qualifying matches at Goodison Park. The atmosphere was superb. For the rest of the matches, like the whole of the country, I was glued to the television.

Mick Jones.

Sheffield United, 1966/67. From left to right, back row: Coldwell, Widdowson, Hodgkinson, G. Shaw. Middle row: Barlow, B. Wagstaff, Munks, Mallender, Matthewson, B. Shaw. Front row: Woodward, Birchenall, Badger, Jones, T. Wagstaff, Reece.

Following England's World Cup triumph, supporters and players around the country could not wait for the new season to start. At Bramall Lane expectation levels were high, with so many youngsters at the club a year wiser and raring to go. It was therefore something of a shock when the opening four League games of the season ended in defeat. Bottom of the table with only one goal scored was not what fans had anticipated.

'A catastrophic start' cited the *Green 'Un*, but reporter Peter Howard was not concerned. 'For me it is inconceivable that the Blades will stay at the bottom. There is too much football there for that to happen.' Howard was correct; the next ten League games would bring six wins, three draws and just one defeat as optimism returned.

As for Mick, after eight blanks he scored his first goal of the season at Sheffield Wednesday in the 'best Sheffield derby for years' according to the *Sheffield Telegraph*. The match at Hillsborough was the 200th between the clubs and finished 2-2. Mick's goal was his first in the fixture. 'No wonder he looked pleased', joked the *Green 'Un*. The next four games brought Mick a further five goals, including a strike against West Brom in a thrilling 4-3 win. The clash against Jimmy Hagan's West Brom team was described as 'tip-top

The 200th derby between Wednesday and United was a cracker!

Mick celebrates after scoring his only goal of this historic match.

entertainment' by the *Sheffield Telegraph*. However, that's what happens when teams 'throw down the gauntlet and go all out to see who can score the most'. Mick was back to his marauding best, 'displaying all the skill and punch at his command in 90 minutes of brilliance'. Tormenting West Brom's defenders, Mick scored once, made two others and caused havoc throughout. 'On this showing there can't be a better leader in the country.'

His manager told local reporters: 'I am not one to moan about bad luck but the ball did not run kindly for us in the opening games. It got so bad the players began to be afraid to try things they would normally not hesitate over, but I always knew we had the ability. Mick

Jones typified the spirit of the side. He went a long time without scoring and was very unhappy about it. He came to see me one morning before the other players arrived; we had a chat and then went out to work on his game. Now he is knocking them in just as we knew he could. That is the type of spirit that has got us over our bad start.'

Talking to the *Sheffield Star* after scoring in a 2-0 win against Sunderland, Mick was delighted, and philosophical.

Sometimes you get the breaks, sometimes you don't. I was not getting them at the start and the tension was building up all the time. I knew it couldn't go on forever. Now I have broken the spell I am feeling a lot happier.

Unfortunately an injury sustained in the win sidelined Mick for six weeks. His absence was not the only one. With Badger, Shaw and Birchenall also out through injury, results suffered; however, as players returned to fitness, performances soon picked up again. Following a 1-1 draw against Arsenal, a match which saw Mick strike his 50th League goal for the club, Harris' youngsters produced a stirring Boxing Day performance to defeat the League's pacesetters Manchester United 2-1, Mick winning the match with a brilliant header in the second half.

It was the team's first win in ten games and Mick's display brought this tribute from his manager when interviewed by the *Sheffield Telegraph*. 'He is now approaching the heading power of Tommy Lawton at his best. Mick has improved tremendously this season, despite his injury problems, and now has the Lawton ability to leap high and hang in the air. I played with and against Lawton. He was difficult to stop, even approach, in the air, and Mick is developing the same sort of skill. Jones, I am sure, will get even better.'

The second half of the season brought some excellent performances. Arguably the best displays came against Fulham, who were thrashed 4-0 (Birchenall and Jones grabbing two goals apiece), and against Sheffield Wednesday, when a Billy Punton strike settled a tight win over their neighbours.

SHEFFIELD UNITED — Colours: Red and White Striped Shirts, Black Shorts

HODGKINSON

2 BADGER   3 SHAW, B.

4 MUNKS   5 MALLENDER   6 WAGSTAFF, B.

FENOUGHTY   BIRCHENALL

7 WOODWARD   8   9 JONES   10   11 PUNTON

Substitute :

Referee : D. LAING, Preston.
Linesmen :
A. BONE, Sunderland (red flag) : W. A. RAINE, Liverpool (yellow flag).

Substitute :

11 BARRETT   9 LEGGAT   7 HAYNES

10 CLARKE   8 BROWN

6 CONWAY   5 CALLAGHAN   4 ROBSON

3 DEMPSEY   2 DRAKE

MACEDO

FULHAM — Colours : White Shirts, Black Shorts.

Spot the future Leeds United star, and England manager, in Fulham's team.

Watch out, Mick's about!

The team also enjoyed their best cup runs since Mick broke into the side, which had fans dreaming of a trip to Wembley, especially in the League Cup before their challenge ended at the quarter-final stage, when, after dominating the tie against Birmingham City, defensive errors proved crucial. In the FA Cup, after defeating Charlton Athletic and

Fulham after a replay, the first game ending 1-1 with goals from Mick and another striker beginning to make a name for himself, Allan Clarke. Sheffield's run ended at Chelsea.

A few weeks after the FA Cup exit, Mick enjoyed probably the most hectic eleven days of his life over the Easter fixtures. Not only did he play five games, but he also found time to get married! His marriage to Glenis Evason at St Leonard's Church, Dinnington brought what seemed the entire village out to celebrate the event. The striker's performances during this period were so impressive he won his place back in the England Under-23 squad. His schedule started with defeats against Arsenal (25 March) and Leeds United (26 and 27 March), before scoring a decisive goal either side of his wedding in wins over Manchester City (1 April) and West Ham (4 April).

Following Mick's display in a 3-0 win over Chelsea in the Blades' penultimate home fixture of the season, some papers began speculating that he was about to win a big-money transfer to champions-elect Manchester United. 'Jones is Busby Target!' was the headline of one national paper. However, whilst flattered he was not looking to move on. The victory over Chelsea would be United's last of the season. Finishing tenth, Mick had enjoyed another tremendous campaign overall, finishing top-scorer for the third consecutive season with 15 league goals.

During the last week of the regular season, Mick won the last of his under-23 caps against Austria. The match saw Mick team up with Fulham's Allan Clarke in attack, the first occasion the duo had played together. Little did either know that within two years they

Match of the Day! It certainly is for Mick and Glenis.

Was Don Revie scouting at this game… England's front two being Clarke and Jones!

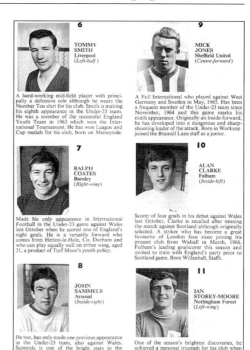

6 TOMMY SMITH Liverpool (*Left-half*)

A hard-working mid-field player with principally a defensive role although he wears the Number Ten shirt for his club. Smith is making his eighth appearance in the Under-23 team. He was a member of the successful England Youth Team in 1963 which won the International Tournament. He has won League and Cup medals for his club, born on Merseyside.

9 MICK JONES Sheffield United (*Centre-forward*)

A Full International who played against West Germany and Sweden in May, 1965. Has been a frequent member of the Under-23 team since November, 1964 and this game marks his ninth appearance. Originally an inside-forward, he has developed into a dangerous and sharp-shooting leader of the attack. Born in Worksop joined the Bramall Lane staff as a junior.

7 RALPH COATES Burnley (*Right-wing*)

Made his only appearance in International Football in the Under-23 game against Wales last October when he scored one of England's eight goals. He is a versatile forward who comes from Hetton-le-Hole, Co. Durham and who can play equally well on either wing, aged 21, a product of Turf Moor's youth policy.

10 ALAN CLARKE Fulham (*Inside-left*)

Scorer of four goals in his debut against Wales last October, Clarke is recalled after missing the match against Scotland although originally selected. A striker who has become a great favourite of London fans since joining his present club from Walsall this season and invited to train with England's party prior to Scotland game. Born Willenhall, Staffs.

8 JOHN SAMMELS Arsenal (*Inside-right*)

He too, has only made one previous appearance in the Under-23 team, also against Wales. Sammels is one of the bright stars in the Arsenal forward line and a frequent goal scorer. He played in the England Youth Team in 1963 and like Tommy Smith was one of the eleven which carried off the trophy at Wembley in the International Tournament that year. Born Ipswich, John is a former Arsenal Junior.

11 IAN STOREY-MOORE Nottingham Forest (*Left-wing*)

One of the season's brightest discoveries, he achieved a personal triumph for his club when he scored all three goals against Everton to win a place in this year's Cup Semi-Final. Played his first Under-23 game against Scotland and seems sure to win further honours in the game. He was born in Ipswich, is aged 22 and made his League debut in 1963.

would form the deadliest partnership around. England won the match with ease 3-0.

England Under-23 v Austria Under-23: Montgomery (Sunderland), Lawler (Liverpool), Thomson (Wolves), Hollins (Chelsea), Mobley (Sheffield Wednesday), Smith (Liverpool), Harvey (Everton), Sammels (Arsenal), Jones (Sheffield United), Clarke (Fulham), Storey-Moore (Nottingham Forest).

Following a brief rest, Mick was travelling again, to South America on the club's post-season tour, though this time for only three weeks, before he could have a well-deserved break following an eventful season.

After playing matches in Chile, Peru and Ecuador, our next venue was Bolivia. We touched down in the middle of a desert; our transport was a rackety old bus. Travelling through the most desolate of regions we saw no buildings or sign of life at all. Eventually we arrived in La Paz, which was built in a volcano! The pitch had sawdust on the lines to mark out the playing area; it was an amazing sight.

A number of players had come down with a bad stomach bug; one was Billy Punton, our left winger. Surprisingly, Billy was down to play. He was obviously not fit, but was in a better shape than some of the others. The manager told Billy to keep breathing fresh air into his lungs. I felt really sorry for him; he was in and out of the toilet as we got changed. As he reappeared, we were due to go out for the match. Billy went out with the manager's message ringing in his ears, 'breath in… breath in'. I kicked off and passed the ball to Tony Wagstaff, who played the ball wide to Billy. As he ran for it he suddenly did a U-turn and headed straight back to the dressing room. He didn't reappear for the rest of the match or any more of our games on the tour!

5

TRANSFER SHENANIGANS
1967/68

Even though there were clear signs that the team was developing, there was a general feeling among supporters that the football club was being held back by cricket, because both sports were played at the ground. The argument had been going on for years, but with football becoming more commercialised, Sheffield United had to move with the times or risk being left behind. The general consensus among fans was that cricket should be played elsewhere and a fourth stand be built. The board was well aware that even though a profit had been made for the previous eight years, attendances were down, and the club could not continue to live off transfer fees.

To compound matters for supporters, there was speculation that Mick Jones would be moving on to one of Division One's bigger clubs. However, the club made it clear

Sheffield United, 1967/68. From left to right, back row: B. Wagstaff, Matthewson, Munks, Hodgkinson, Mallender, Widdowson, Birchenall, Barlow, Shaw. Front row: Hill, Woodward, T. Wagstaff, Jones, Badger, Reece, Cliff, Fenoughty.

in a newspaper report on 6 August that he wasn't for sale 'at any price'. Sheffield began the season poorly, with just one win being gained in the opening eight League matches. Following heavy defeats against Arsenal and Manchester City, rumours of Mick's departure surfaced again.

From time to time there were snippets in the papers saying different teams were interested in me, but I ignored them, because I was happy at Sheffield United. The club had been good to me and the supporters had been excellent, which meant a lot because I've seen players who don't have that support really struggle. At the beginning of the season Leeds United appeared to be interested in me. Before we played Manchester City a reporter at the game told me that their manager, Don Revie, was watching me, but I thought nothing of it; he could be watching anyone.

The first report of significance was on Monday 18 September, when the *Sheffield Star* reported that 'neither Don Revie nor John Harris would comment on the latest rumours of Jones' switch to Leeds United'. Previously the club had been quick to crush any suggested interest in their prize assets. The silence at both grounds was worrying the *Star*. 'Do United want First Division greatness? Or do they want mediocrity and a "good nursery" tag? Kill this Jones story Blades... and kill it now.'

Keith Farnsworth, writing in the *Sheffield Telegraph* the following morning, also believed that both clubs' silence spoke volumes. According to Farnsworth, both Francis Lee of Bolton and Clive Clark of West Brom were also on Revie's wanted list. With his own team struggling for goals, Leeds were about to make a 'big splash in the transfer market'. He concluded that with Sheffield rooted to the bottom of the table club officials were now actively looking for immediate replacements, even if it meant selling 'the Lane's greatest asset since Jimmy Hagan'.

On Thursday 21 September a Board meeting and Football Committee meeting was scheduled to take place at Bramall Lane. Club chairman Mr Blacow Yates had informed local reporters on 19 September that 'Mick Jones is not on the agenda for the board meeting. Whether or not the subject arises in "other business" I cannot say. In any event it is a matter for consideration by the Football Committee meeting, which immediately follows the full meeting of the board.' The committee's chairman Mr Dick Wragg was 'out of town' but would be back for the meeting.

Farnsworth noted in the *Sheffield Telegraph* that the meeting would be one of the 'most dramatic' in the clubs history. 'Eleven men are set to play the "match" of a lifetime.' Having signed Willie Carlin earlier in the week, the £100,000 bid for Jones would solve a number of issues. The result of the meetings was that Leeds United's offer was acceptable.

The following morning, Mr Wragg, Don Revie and Mr Albert Morris, Leeds United's chairman, met to finalise a deal. Meanwhile, John Harris was putting the finishing

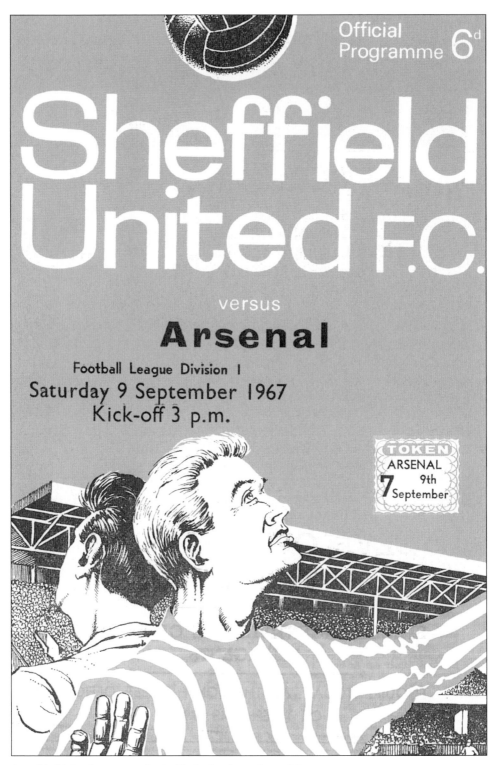

A goal in his last home game for the Blades, but Arsenal won 4-2.

CITY

VERSUS

SHEFFIELD UNITED

SEASON
1967-68

MANCHESTER CITY F.C.,
MAINE ROAD, MANCHESTER.
LEAGUE DIVISION 1 CHAMPIONSHIP.

SATURDAY, 16th SEPTEMBER 1967
Kick-off 3-0 p.m.

OFFICIAL PROGRAMME 1/-

Another defeat – it also turned out to be Mick Jones's last game for Sheffield United.

touches to his team selection for the following day's match with Newcastle United. As far he was concerned, his centre forward would be playing, confirming his views to the press. 'Mick is still a Sheffield United player. I must assume that he is available to play for us tomorrow until I hear otherwise.' (It is clear that Harris was opposed to the transfer, as he admitted in an interview with the *Green 'Un* on 13 April 1968, but there was little he could do.)

After concluding their negotiations, Revie and Morris went round to their target's home to complete the transfer, but had to wait because he was out shopping at a local supermarket with his wife!

The papers were full of rumours all week, but nobody at Sheffield United told me about any of the negotiations with Leeds United. I went in for training throughout the week and continued to have treatment on an ankle injury. On the Friday, Joe Shaw said to me 'you should get yourself off to Leeds lad, it would be a good move for you'.

John Harris had picked me to play against Newcastle United the following day, but I was feeling unsettled. I was determined to find out what was going on. John Harris didn't know, but he arranged for me to see Mr Wragg, who told me they'd been offered £100,000, which was a lot of money and the board had decided to accept it. They had given Leeds permission to speak to me. It was now up to me. I left Bramall Lane stunned.

I picked up Glenis to do some shopping but on our return home there was commotion at our house. All I could see was television cameras and newspapermen; it was heaving. Neither of us had any idea what was going on. Then I saw Don Revie with Albert Morris, the club's chairman. I had a quick word with one of the photographers, who told me Revie was here to sign me.

After introducing themselves, Don asked me if I was ambitious. Of course I was. He told me he'd wanted to sign me for a while. We went into the house; Don told me about his plans and vision for the club. It didn't take me long to sign. My wages increased but money never motivated me as a player; it was ambition I was after and Leeds could offer me that.

Suddenly, Mick Jones was the costliest player ever sold by Sheffield United and the costliest ever bought by Leeds United. At the same time he was only the third £100,000 footballer in Britain, and quickly gave his thoughts to waiting reporters.

I am very conscious of leaving the Bramall Lane crowd and hope I get as good a one at Leeds, but it will take a while to settle in. I didn't want to leave my mates but it was too good an offer to turn down. I never asked for a transfer, but, obviously, I want to get on and this is a big chance. I only wish I could have said goodbye to Mr Harris.

Revie also spoke for the first time of the club's record transfer. 'I have been interested in Mick for a year. He is a strong lad and has that goal flair. We have been creating a lot of chances and we are hoping he is going to knock them in, but I hope our fans won't expect it all to happen straightaway.' Leeds chairman Mr Morris smiled and said: 'It's the biggest transfer we have been associated with and I hope it's one club record that will never have to be beaten.'

With a strong reaction from supporters expected, Mr Wragg's comments were strictly official. 'This was done as a decision of the Football Committee and as a member of that committee I support it.' As for John Harris, he would make no comment on his immediate future, but suggested he would quit. As anticipated the reaction from supporters was strong. Letters flooded in to local newspapers, criticising the club for a 'lack of ambition'. Some fans even followed their hero to his new club! Initially, John Harris resigned before being persuaded to reconsider. He was eventually re-appointed. However, whilst Sheffield United had their own problems to sort out, Mick Jones had a new career ahead of him following the events of an extraordinary day.

I found out later that Arsenal, Manchester United and Leeds had all enquired about me at varying times, but had been turned down because John wanted to keep all the young players he'd developed together. It was a sad day for Sheffield United, but I was not the only one to leave that season, Alan Birchenall joined Chelsea. I felt sorry for supporters who'd been going for years because suddenly the promising team they had seen assembled really struggled. At the end of the 1967/68 season they finished bottom, and it took a while for them to return.

Sheffield United had given me my start in football, and without John Harris and his coaching staff I would not have developed so quickly. The club's youth policy enabled numerous players to break into top-flight football sooner than they could have expected, and during my time at Bramall Lane I'd won international honours. Whenever I return to Bramall Lane, I am always well received because supporters remember the effort I gave during matches. However, in the late sixties certain clubs were more ambitious than Sheffield United – Leeds United was one of them.

Everyone in the game knew Leeds was an up-and-coming club, they'd been close to winning honours a few times and clearly had ambition. I drove over to Leeds that night and started to feel the pressure, because I was now a £100,000 player and there were very few of those in the country at the time. Having said that, I was incredibly excited. Although I hadn't trained for two weeks, I was down to make my debut the next day against Leicester City. I had a medical before reporting to the Craiglands Hotel in Ilkley, where the players stayed before every match. When I arrived at the hotel, the players were playing carpet bowls. I was introduced to them, and I roomed with Billy Bremner that night.

The atmosphere was electric. You could sense the set-up was right, the players were being assembled and things were about to take off. As a player, I wanted to win a League title and the FA Cup, at Leeds it was clear that I could. Everything I'd worked for was now possible. Next morning there were more tests down at the hospital. Afterwards I joined the players for a pre-match meal. At the team meeting, Don told me to ignore the transfer fee, just play as I normally did.

Mick received a number of good luck telegrams, including one from John Harris before his debut game, which Leeds came from behind to win 3-2. Despite failing to score, he played a part in two of the goals, and had a couple of headers brilliantly saved by the 'keeper. In addition, as far as the *Yorkshire Post* was concerned 'the sight of Jones and Jack Charlton in the same penalty area for Leeds' corners is enough to strike fear in the hearts of the best defences'.

The *Yorkshire Post* was certainly impressed with the new boy: 'Jones did enough on his debut to show why the whole town will shortly be talking about him… In the air

All the best from the ex-boss.

№ 06226

LEEDS UNITED A.F.C TOKEN

Leicester City 10 1967-1968

OFFICIAL PROGRAMME ONE SHILLING

VERSUS

LEICESTER CITY

SATURDAY, 23rd SEPTEMBER, 1967 K.O. 3 p.m.

NEXT HOME MATCHES

SATURDAY, 30th SEPTEMBER, K.O. 3 p.m.   C.L.

BURNLEY RESERVES

SATURDAY, 7th OCTOBER K.O. 3 p.m.   F.L.

CHELSEA

An exciting debut, Leeds won 3-2.

he was impeccable, on the ground far from cumbersome, and often ultra-intelligent. In all it is a display with which he can be well satisfied.' Revie told the paper: 'I thought Mick was great. Considering the tense situation he did very well right from the start and was getting up well in the air, not only in front of goal. He showed his authority in this respect all right.'

We won the match but I was a bit disappointed with my performance even though Don Revie told me I'd done fine. After the match Ronnie Hilton, who produced a number of Leeds records, congratulated me, as did Morecambe and Wise, which delighted me because I loved their brand of comedy, second only to Laurel and Hardy.

The opening weeks of Mick's career at Elland Road was at times a struggle, although he played in a couple of high scoring victories over Chelsea 7-0 and Spora Luxembourg 9-0; the latter game bringing him his first goal for the club. His strike, the ninth of the match, broke a twenty-nine-year-old club record.

Mick's first League goal for Leeds arrived on 4 November in a 3-1 win over Arsenal. The build up to the goal followed sustained pressure when Mick forced a brilliant save from Arsenal 'keeper Jim Furnell. From the corner, he forced another save but fell awkwardly whilst challenging for the cross. Although limping, his third header, from a second corner, gave the 'keeper no chance for his first League goal, but it had been at a price. At half-time he was substituted.

In an interview with the *Yorkshire Post*, his manager was not concerned. 'Jones injured his ankle in his last game for Sheffield United, so he has done no training other than routine body exercises since he arrived here. He has also been looking for a new house in this district and with his wife expecting a baby, under the circumstances I am pleased that he has done as well as he has. The injury is not a serious one but it was aggravated in the goalmouth activity which led to his goal, and it would be foolish to risk the possibility of it getting worse.'

Revie added: 'I cannot praise him too highly for his attitude since he joined us. He has had one slice of ill luck after another. He has had an injury, and has constantly gone over on it, but he has played whenever I have asked him and he has given everything. His courage has been a tremendous example to the rest of the side and in the highest traditions of what we have come to expect from the players. Mick has been no more than sixty per cent fit since he joined us. Even at that our money was well spent. We haven't seen the best of him, but we will.'

After almost two months on the sidelines, Mick returned against Wolves on 23 December and scored in his side's 2-1 win. His return coincided with a run of six consecutive wins, with more goals coming against Fulham, Southampton and Everton. The run would continue into April as the team put together a fourteen-match unbeaten run.

№ 09342

OFFICIAL PROGRAMME
ONE SHILLING

LEEDS UNITED A.F.C. TOKEN

ARSENAL 19 1967-1968

VERSUS

ARSENAL

SATURDAY, 4th NOVEMBER, 1967   **K.O. 3 p.m.**

NEXT HOME MATCHES

WEDNESDAY, 8th NOVEMBER K.O. 7-30 p.m.   F.L.

MANCHESTER UNITED

SATURDAY, 11th NOVEMBER, K.O. 3 p.m.   C.L.

BARNSLEY RESERVES

LEEDS UNITED FOOTBALL POOL

are you a member?
IF NOT! JOIN NOW

enquiries to
THE POOLS OFFICE, 1 OXFORD PLACE LEEDS 1 and at THE POOLS KIOSK WEST STAND CAR PARK

At last… Mick's first League goal came in this clash.

Mick in the white of Leeds, 1967.

Yorkshire Evening Post's cartoonist educates Leeds followers on their record signing.

Following the 5-0 demolition of Fulham, one newspaper noted: 'It was men against boys… skilled, no-frills professionalism against which so many players looked like… novices. When £100,000 Leeds centre forward Jones got his first goal he dribbled out of his own half past four men before drawing Macedo out to leave him floundering too. If Jones had edged his way through saying "Excuse me" I wouldn't have been surprised, so meek was Fulham's acquiescence.'

This period saw Leeds make progress in three other competitions. They looked unstoppable in pursuit of major honours. Cup-tied, Mick watched his teammates reach the League Cup final. A week before the final, an article appeared in the *Yorkshire Evening Post* titled 'Mick Jones on top of the world with Leeds'. It was one of the first major interviews Mick had given since his record-breaking transfer.

My game has improved, but then it had to playing in a side like this. Mr Revie has a very strong pool of players. Eighteen of us train together, and all of us are fighting for a First Division place. It may be a big pool as far as a lot of clubs go but it pays off. I have always thought the real strength of any side lies in its middle line. Here we have Billy Bremner, Jack Charlton and Norman Hunter, to say nothing of players like Paul Madeley. The Bremner-Johnny Giles link is fabulous. Giles is the best link-man in the game, his work-rate is fantastic.

Leeds don't build just one system, they have players who can slot in all over the place. I am in there to take weight off other people, but it works the other way. No one slings a high ball up the middle and just leaves me to get on with it. Someone is always looking for ways to help you out. I'm a more confident player since I came here. Leeds set a high standard. They are very ambitious and we are all dying to win something for the boss. It's every player's ambition to play at Wembley, but I think most of all we would like to win the Championship. When you sit down and think about it that's the one that takes most winning. You have to be so consistent. We are playing well and showing no signs of staleness after all the matches we have had... We must win something with a pool like ours.

The League Cup final may have been a drab affair, but Terry Cooper's first half strike was sufficient to beat Arsenal and finally remove the 'bridesmaid' label from Revie's team. In the FA Cup, wins over Derby County, Nottingham Forest, Bristol City and his old club Sheffield United, saw Leeds into the semi-finals. Mick scored in the

Mick strikes against Nottingham Forest in a fourth round FA Cup tie at Elland Road.

matches against Forest and Bristol, however, the games would be best remembered for the performances of Leeds' deputy goalkeepers!

Against Nottingham Forest, Gary Sprake got injured and had to go off for a spell, Norman Hunter deputised. Forest scored before Gary returned, but we eventually won the match 2-1. Against Bristol, we were winning 2-0 when Gary got involved in an incident with Chris Garland and got sent off. This time Peter Lorimer went in, and did quite well. Big Jack and Norman protected him well though!

By the time Leeds faced Everton in the semi-finals, they were still in with a chance of winning the League, despite losing to Stoke City a few days before the clash at Old Trafford. Sadly, one incredible mistake from Sprake proved costly in Leeds pursuit of a second Wembley visit in a season.

I was devastated because I'd never played in a cup final, as for Gary's error it wasn't the first time he'd make a big-match blunder.

When Leeds faced Liverpool in a crucial League encounter at Elland Road on 4 May they knew a victory was vital. Don Revie's described the match as 'the most important in the club's history'. After giving Leeds the lead, two goals in a couple of minutes swung the match Liverpool's way. Tom Holley in the *Yorkshire Post* concluded that, 'it was absolute fatigue, both mentally and physically that caught up with Leeds in their 63rd game of a hectic season'.

Following the defeat Revie rested a number of players as Leeds attempted to reach a second successive Inter-Cities Fairs Cup final. During an impressive run, Leeds had defeated Spora Luxembourg easily, before accounting for Partizan Belgrade, Hibernian and Rangers in tight encounters. They now faced Scottish opponents for the third time… Dundee.

Leeds squeezed through to the final 2-1 on aggregate, but it had been close. Phil Browne in the *Yorkshire Evening Post* was delighted despite the fact that the team was 'completely played out mentally and physically by their mammoth programme… To force any more competitive games on them would be football cruelty to a side that a few weeks back could have taken on any team in Europe.'

When we played Dundee in the second leg of the Fairs Cup, I knew that this was my last chance of winning honours that season. I missed the first leg in Scotland, which we drew 1-1, so was looking forward to this match. It was a really tight game, and it was far from vintage football, but we reached the final thanks to a goal from Eddie Gray. The actual final was delayed due to a backlog of games until August, so during the summer break I was able to reflect on an extraordinary season for myself.

Another cup goal, this time in the FA Cup fifth round against Bristol City.

Cartoon fun before an all-Yorkshire quarter-final clash.

A Sprake blunder cost Leeds dear.

Leeds attack during their Fairs Cup clash with Rangers.

I could not have had a better beginning to my professional career, but at Leeds the difference in attitudes and aspirations was incredible. They were so professional in their outlook. At Sheffield we travelled by coach to Southampton; to conserve energy and time at Leeds we flew. More thought seemed to be put into things. Of course, Sheffield's players and management team wanted to be successful, but the set-up at Leeds was on a different scale. Everything was geared to success from the top down; the attention to detail was amazing. It was like a time bomb waiting to explode.

The belief and determination to succeed amongst the players was incredible. It was clear Don wanted to develop a team that could challenge for honours regularly both in Division One and in Europe. The atmosphere, culture and ethos he had developed was fantastic. Nothing was taken to chance.

I was bought to score goals, but there were other sides to my game that helped the team, and Don knew this. My first season was a period of adjusting. There were

Mick in action, 1968.

After their FA Cup disappointment, Leeds made no mistake in the Fairs Cup.

Time to relax – at home with Glenis and Lindsey.

world-class players at Elland Road, but I didn't feel overawed, after all, the boss had been willing to pay £100,000 for me. I wanted to be successful and I was willing to work, so I soon fitted in. Nobody thought they were better than anyone else was, we were a team and appreciated what we all brought. Life could not have been better.

6

CHAMPIONS
1968/69

The opening game of the 1968/69 campaign was the delayed first leg of the previous seasons Fairs Cup final. With the match occurring in the middle of a local bank holiday and coverage live on television (rare in the 1960s), the gate was affected, with just over 25,000 fans attending.

Leeds United v Ferencvaros, 1968 Fairs Cup final first leg:

Leeds United: Sprake, Reaney, Cooper, Bremner (captain), Charlton, Hunter, Lorimer, Madeley, Jones (sub. Belfitt), Giles (sub. Greenhoff), Gray
Ferencvaros: Geczi, Novak, Pancsics, Havasi, Szucs, Juhasz, Szoke, Varga, Albert, Rakosi, Fenyvesi (sub. Balint)

Ferencvaros relied on the counter-attack as Leeds tried to break down a nine-man defence. The goal just before half-time was controversial. Lorimer floated a corner under the Ferencvaros bar; Geczi went up for the ball, but missed it completely, having been put off by Charlton. Charlton then touched the ball on for Jones to force the ball over the line. As Leeds tried in vain for a second, Ferencvaros nearly grabbed an equaliser at the end, but Sprake saved brilliantly from Rakosi.

Phil Browne of the *Yorkshire Evening Post* was concerned. 'That old enemy of Leeds United's faulty finishing leaves them with a hard row to hoe at Budapest against Ferencvaros in the deciding second leg of the Fairs Cup final, but so often have found their best form when facing high odds… that all may be well.'

Speaking with the *Yorkshire Post* after the game, Don Revie was far from happy with Ferencvaros's tactics. 'They were body checking, deliberately handling and obstructing … Some of it was diabolically clever and screened. Mick Jones has been lucky. He was kicked in the groin and it is sore, but it could have been worse. It will be tough now in Budapest but we have faced tough ones before. We would have liked a two-goal lead, but keeping a clean sheet was an achievement.'

Against Ferencvaros I had to take some punishment. As the target-man I always expected a tough game, but the Hungarians were really cynical. I remember an incident with their goalkeeper Geczi when we both went for a fifty-fifty ball. As I went

Yorkshire Evening Post Fairs Cup final special.

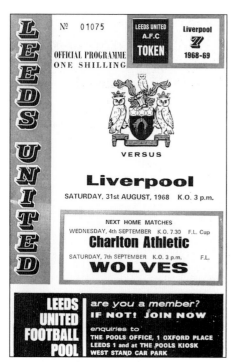

Left: It was tight, but Mick's header proved the difference. Right: Up for the Cup!

for the ball he came out and jumped up with his leg in the air and hit me straight in the middle. I thought he'd broken me in two. Luckily, I jack-knifed to take the blow instead of taking the hit straight in the stomach. Nowadays he'd have been sent off, but he got away with it. I was carried off. It was a good result though because we hadn't conceded an away goal. Naturally, I was pleased to score our goal, even if it was scrappy, poking the ball in from about two yards with a number of defenders around me, but it was one of the most important goals I scored for Leeds. It gave us something to take into the second leg.

Leeds began their League Division One campaign in terrific style, winning their opening four fixtures against Southampton, Queen's Park Rangers, Stoke City and Ipswich Town. Following the win over Stoke, Tom Holley in the *Yorkshire Post* felt that 'Jones looks more and more like his £100,000 tag as he kept up his goal-a-game record'.

We started really well and I was knocking a few goals in, including a header against Liverpool which I was particularly pleased with to settle a really tight game. We were among the pacesetters.

The players turned their attentions back to the Fairs Cup.

Nº 14360

**OFFICIAL PROGRAMME
ONE SHILLING**

LEEDS UNITED
A.F.C
TOKEN

Ferencvaros
1
1968-69

VERSUS

Ferencvaros

INTER CITIES FAIRS CUP FINAL — 1st LEG

WEDNESDAY, 7th AUGUST, 1968   K.O. 7.30 p.m.

NEXT HOME MATCHES

SATURDAY, 10th AUGUST   K.O. 3 p.m.   C.L.

Blackburn Rovers Res

WEDNESDAY, 14th AUGUST   K.O. 7.30 p.m.   F.L.

QUEENS PARK RANGERS

Advantage Leeds, following the first leg.

All eyes on the ball as Lorimer's corner is floated over.

Despite five defenders, Mick squeezes the ball home.

Flat out – but Leeds are a goal to the good.

Come on ref!

Mick's final is over following Ferencvaros 'keeper Geczi's challenge.

Ferencvaros v Leeds United, 1968 Fairs Cup final second leg:

Ferencvaros: Geczi, Novak, Pancsics, Havasi, Szucs, Juhasz, Szoke (sub. Kraba), Varga, Albert, Rakosi, Katona
Leeds United: Sprake, Reaney, Cooper, Bremner (captain), Charlton, Hunter, O'Grady, Lorimer, Jones, Madeley, Hibbitt (sub. Bates)

In the second leg Gary Sprake was magnificent. Over the years he's had a lot of stick for his errors in crucial matches, however in Budapest when we were really under the cosh, Gary was sensational. He made a number of world-class saves and won us the cup that night.

After the game, Revie was relieved: 'I tried everything I knew to inject confidence in the players, but I was more than a little worried about the outcome of the return. When we got into those final few minutes my heart nearly stopped beating. As the final whistle drew nearer every minute seemed like an hour.'

The team quite rightly received praise from the media.

Frank McGhee, *The Mirror*: 'Leeds at last have fought their way into British football's hall of fame – they can now point to a trophy every club in Europe would be proud to possess.'

R.H. Williams, *Daily Telegraph*: 'If 0-0 suggests a boring war of attrition it could not be more misleading... Leeds were engaged in the battle of their lives against a fast, fluent and clever Hungarian side who would probably have humbled any other defence in the world.'

Alan Thompson, *Daily Express*: 'Fingernails may need a manicure, all adrenaline has been drained and the heart has taken a hammering, but Leeds, those masters of deep and discipline defence, held out against an onslaught of green-shirted Hungarians that lasted for almost the entirety of this game. How they did it is something of a miracle.'

Phil Browne, *Yorkshire Evening Post*: 'One of the most exciting goal-less draws ever played... the defence, famous as it has become, had its finest hour.'

The Fairs Cup triumph was my first major honour as a player, so I was naturally delighted. When I started out as a professional, winning the League and FA Cup were the major targets, Europe was not really a consideration, so to win such a prestigious honour was incredible. When we returned to the dressing room the celebrations were fantastic, as was the journey home. Back in Leeds we had a civic reception at the Town Hall. There were thousands lining the streets to greet us, it was a wonderful sight.

Returning triumphantly, Leeds ran out in front of a packed house at Elland Road to face League-leaders Arsenal, looking for their seventh consecutive win. In a thrilling encounter, Leeds won 2-0. Tom Holley of the *Yorkshire Post* was impressed. 'Don Revie's cherished ambition to win the League title took a giant step forward in this battle of the First Division 'toppers'. There is still a long way to go, but on this form I cannot see anyone to beat them... Leeds were tighter in defence, superior in midfield and more penetrative in attack, through Jones' Herculean efforts.'

Undefeated, Leeds travelled to Maine Road to play the defending champions, but slipped to a 3-1 defeat. Disappointed, the players immediately bounced back with three wins, before a crushing 5-1 defeat at Burnley. This would be the team's last reverse of the season, although it was also the start of a worrying eight-game spell that would yield only three wins and seven goals.

We weren't concerned because we knew the goals would come, and in any case we were conceding very few. Everything clicked when we played the return fixture against Burnley. We hammered them 6-1. I was particularly pleased because I hadn't scored for a couple of months and managed to grab a goal. Scoring is all about confidence, and that game was the start of a tremendous run for me.

Tom Holley, *Yorkshire Post*, was full of praise following the demolition of Burnley. 'After this magnificent display who can doubt that Leeds are still capable of brilliant attacking football? In a terrific first half "blitz" they took Burnley by the scruff of the neck to hand out a real spanking.'

The magnificent eleven. From left to right, back row: Hunter, Bates, Madeley, Sprake, Charlton, O'Grady. Front row: Cooper, Bremner, Reaney, Jones, Lorimer.

Celebration time.

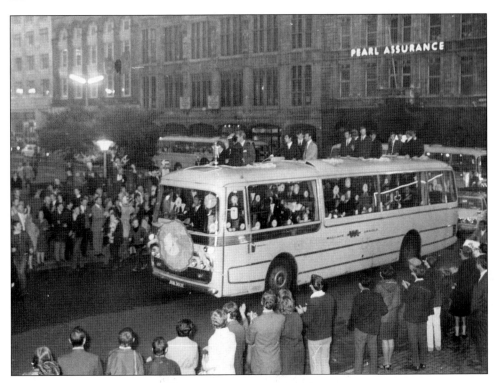

The boys are back in town… with the Fairs Cup.

Leeds United, 1968/69. From left to right, back row: Reaney, Charlton, Madeley, Jones, Harvey, Sprake, Belfitt, Gray, Hunter. Front row: Hibbitt, Giles, Cooper, Bremner, O'Grady, Bates, Lorimer, Johanneson.

The biggest cheer of the match went to Mick, who scored his first goal since 9 October. Don Revie was delighted with his centre forward's efforts. 'I don't care if Mick fails to score again this season… he does his fair share of creating the openings for others. He is one of the most unselfish players I have seen, always willing to take the knocks and wait to let someone else through. There is not a better clubman in the game.'

High flyer – Mick gets the better of two Sheffield Wednesday defenders.

The turning point of the season as Leeds hammer Burnley.

The victory over Burnley was one of the key games during the season. It was the start of an eleven-game run, when Leeds won ten matches, seven consecutively, placing Revie's team in pole position to clinch a Division One title for the first time. Among a number of notable triumphs was a 1-0 win at QPR, before Leeds finally overhauled Liverpool at the top of the table on 12 February after a 2-0 win over Ipswich Town. The win against QPR was important because Leeds were three points behind with two games in hand; a loss would have put immense pressure on them. Two games later, following the win over Ipswich, Leeds were top by a point, but crucially it was the first time since the early stages of the season that both teams had played the same number of games.

Unlike the previous season we had no distractions in the cups, Ujpest Dozsa ended our defence of the Fairs Cup at the quarter-final stage; and we had already made early exits in both the FA Cup and League Cup. All our efforts were now on the run-in to the title.

When Stoke City were hammered 5-1 on 8 March, the last of seven consecutive League wins, the lead had been doubled over their only challengers Liverpool. According to national papers, the title race was over. 'Follow that!' headlined one tabloid.

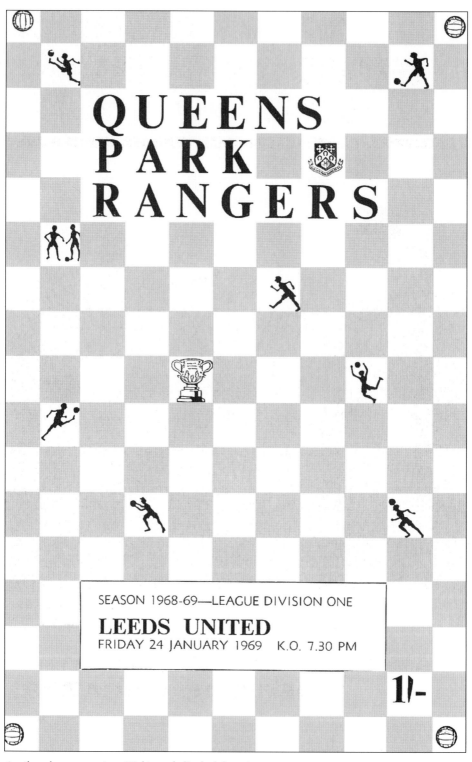

Another close encounter – Mick's goal clinched the points.

THE CERAMIC CITY *CLIPPER*

You put your right foot out !—Harry Burrows and Albion's Tony Brown do a version of the Hokey-Cokey, a dance onlooker Micky Bernard will be too young to remember – Picture: **Jack Brindley**, Stoke City Times.

STOKE CITY FOOTBALL CLUB

OFFICIAL MAGAZINE

Vol. 1 No. 18

PRICE 1/-

Leeds go 'nap' at the Victoria Ground.

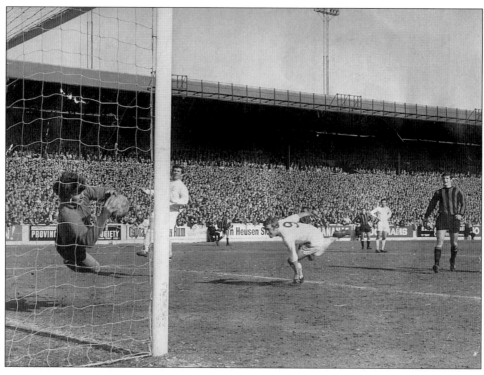

Mick goes close in a clash against Manchester City.

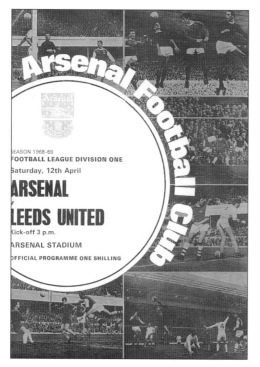

'"We are the Champions!" roared the army of day-trippers from Elland Road before the game started. Ninety minutes, five goals, and two points later, even that hard-to-convince gentlemen Bill Shankly would have been struggling to put together any kind of case for his beloved Liverpool.'

After the game, Stoke manager Tony Waddington commented, 'They murdered us. There isn't a better-equipped side in the country. If they have weaknesses, they are so well disguised you can't find them. When people say they are a dull side without flair, I feel amused. It is inconceivable to imagine them failing this time.'

Leeds' 2-1 win at Highbury was a crucial victory.

Mick scores a crucial header against Leicester during the run-in.

Recent campaigns, however, meant that the players and Revie were taking nothing for granted, a point proved when the next four games resulted in three draws and just one victory, against Manchester City. However, wins over Arsenal 2-1 and Leicester City 2-0 took the team to within touching distance of the title. For Revie, the win at Highbury was arguably the 'best of the season'. Leeds were the only side to record a 'double' over the Gunners that season and the result, according to the Leeds manager, was a 'blow to Liverpool's hopes that we might fall apart in our remaining fixtures.'

Our wins over Arsenal and Leicester were so crucial because the tension was beginning to mount as we got closer to the title. At Highbury, Gary got into a fight after a few minutes with Bobby Gould and was lucky to stay on the field after punching him. Ian Ure was marking me that day, and we had a real battle. I scored the first when a long ball was played out of defence. He had a few yards on me but my pace caught him out and I rattled the ball home with my left foot. John Giles scored a tap-in for our second, which gave us a great win. A week later I scored with a header against Leicester at Elland Road, Eddie Gray added a second which set us up nicely for the final few games.

A 0-0 draw at Everton (a match Mick missed due to flu) three days later took Leeds to within a point of the title, as Liverpool's clash at Coventry also ended scoreless. On

28 April, the players went back to Merseyside for an encounter with Liverpool at Anfield. It is a game that Mick will never forget.

We went to Liverpool knowing that a draw would win us the League Championship; it could not have been a harder place to go. Even though we had another game left, we wanted to clinch the title at our greatest rivals. Don told us to get out there and do the business; we all knew what was at stake. We were nervous but went out feeling confident. It was a really tough match, they had a few near misses and we also went close on a couple of occasions, but we defended well and fully deserved our draw to win the League. We were all ecstatic.

Nothing, however, could have prepared the players for the crowd's reaction at the end of the match.

As we were coming off the pitch, Don waved us towards the Kop. We felt a bit uneasy about this, but slowly walked towards this mass of fans and stood in a line in front of the Kop and clapped them. Suddenly someone got on top of someone else's shoulders and started chanting 'Champions, Champions...' Incredibly, the whole Kop joined in; the noise was deafening. All you could see was a mass of red and white scarves acclaiming us as the Champions. It was a fantastic sight and sound that I will never forget. Liverpool supporters were always known for their sportsmanship – that night they showed what fantastic fans they are.

Unbeknown to us Don had hidden crates of champagne and beer in the coach; it was waiting for us when we got back to the dressing room. Bill Shankly came in to congratulate us all despite his own personal disappointment, but that didn't surprise me because we had a great respect for each other as clubs and over the years we had some fantastic battles. Fortunately we won the crucial ones, not only that night, but also in a Fairs Cup semi-final encounter in 1971 and an FA Cup clash a year later. The celebrations after were fantastic. It was some evening!

Don Revie was jubilant. 'Winning the Championship makes me very glad for the players as well as for the rest of us… All the team's fine character showed up. Liverpool came at us very hard and fast, but our men absorbed their effort like Champions can, and then they gave as good as Liverpool had given. It would have been sweet to win the title at home, but if we had to win it away, then I am glad it has been done at Anfield. What a place to triumph at and what a crowd for generosity.'

Following the club's success, which made them Yorkshire's fourth club to win the Division One title since 1929/30, the media was unanimous in their praise of Leeds United.

Barry Foster, *Yorkshire Post*: 'It has taken the most consistent performance in the history of the League in the end to win the title. Leeds have recorded the fewest defeats

The crunch match – a point and the First Division title would go to Leeds.

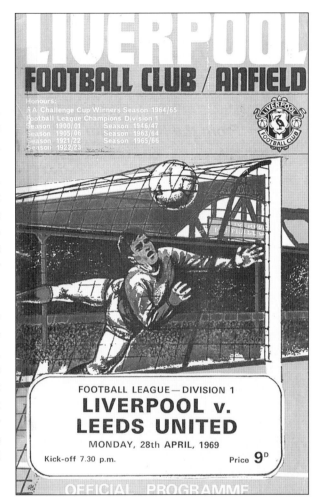

ever in a First Division campaign, mainly due to the relentless way which Liverpool have tracked them. Last night, Liverpool's challenge ended when they failed to break down the Leeds defence which surpassed many of its famous feats in Europe in the way it shrugged off wave after wave of attacks...'

Donald Saunders, *Daily Telegraph*: 'Who could justly begrudge the dedicated, superbly efficient professionals from Elland Road their first success in this, the most demanding of all soccer competitions? Now, they have achieved their objective and earned nationwide respect.'

Derek Wallis, *Daily Mirror*:
'There has been no doubt in my mind for two seasons that Leeds are the best equipped of all English teams for the traps, tensions and special demands of the competition they will now enter – the European Cup. Leeds United are the champions, the masters, the new kings of English football – at last.'

Phil Browne, *Yorkshire Evening Post*: 'It was not a game for the faint hearted, but for all its fierceness it was sportingly played. In a season when bookings have been ten a penny, it was good to see this crucial match decently played, and the vast Anfield Kop give its own thunderous tribute at the end... that told United they deserved the point which had brought them their first Championship. The steely stuff of which Champions are made was easily seen in United as they delivered their quiet knockout blow.'

Two days later, Leeds played Nottingham Forest at Elland Road in front of a sell-out crowd, and ended the season with a 1-0 win (John Giles scored the only goal after eighty-five minutes) which enabled them to set a host of records. Most points in a season (67); most home points (39); most wins (27); most home wins (18); fewest defeats (2), also fewest away defeats; fewest goals conceded (26) and fewest goals conceded at home (9).

Leeds United League record: P42 W 27 D 13 L 2 F 66 A 26 Pts 67.

Player appearances during the season (substitute in brackets): Sprake 42, Reaney 42, Cooper 34(1), Bremner 42, Charlton 41, Hunter 42, Lorimer 25(4), O'Grady 38, Jones 40, Giles 32, Gray 32(1), Madeley 31, Hibbitt 9(3), Belfitt 6(2), Bates 3(1), Greenhoff 3, Johannesson 0(1).

Goals: Jones 14, Lorimer 9, O'Grady 8, Giles 8, Bremner 6, Gray 5, Charlton 3, Madeley 3, Belfitt 3, Hibbitt 3, Johannesson 1, Cooper 1, Reaney 1, own goal 1.

The Championship triumph and season overall – Mick's first full campaign at the club – had been sensational.

I have so many memories from that season, but naturally the match at Anfield, the reception from the Kop, the dressing room celebrations, the carnival atmosphere against Nottingham Forest after the presentation of the trophy and the civic reception, when thousands turned out, are moments I will never forget. Overall though it was the achievement of winning the Championship that meant most.

Mick evades Liverpool 'hard man' Tommy Smith during a gripping encounter.

Kop that! Leeds players receive the applause from the Anfield faithful.

All smiles – Leeds have done it.

We are the Champions! Leeds celebrate winning the title following the presentation of the Championship Trophy after their win over Nottingham Forest.

Yorkshire Evening Post cartoonist Speed's tribute to the new champs.

The squad that Don built.

To win a League medal was the pinnacle for a player. The FA Cup, which has the tradition and is the greatest cup competition in the world is fantastic, but you can have a reasonable draw and before you know it you're in the latter stages, and it's not always the best side that wins each season. In the League, however, you cannot get away with anything. Over a season, you play everybody in different conditions, and if you come out top there is no denying you are the best in that particular campaign.

You need consistency and must be able to overcome injuries. If you win the League you are the best side in the country, any professional footballer will tell you that, and it's the one every player wants to win. For me that triumph stands out, it was my first Championship medal and is something I was very proud to achieve. To cap a great season, I also finished the League campaign as top scorer with 14 goals.

The 1968/69 campaign was a tremendous achievement and we knew more success would follow. The team had matured and was one of the most feared around.

7

TREBLE HEARTBREAK
1969/70

Leeds may have just been crowned Champions, but Don Revie was not prepared to rest, he wanted to move forward. In seven years he had taken the club from obscurity to the pinnacle of English football. His signing of Allan Clarke for a British record fee of £165,000 served notice to every club that Leeds United would be the team to beat for the foreseeable future. Revie believed that pairing the rapier-like Clarke with Jones as the target man would prove a devastating partnership.

The new strike-force made their first appearance together in the Charity Shield against Manchester City. Although neither scored in the 2-1 win, the potential was obvious for

Household names, August 1969. From left to right: Lorimer, Charlton, Clarke, Jones, Gray, Madeley, Cooper, Hunter, Giles, Reaney, Sprake, Bremner.

Mick races clear from Mick Summerbee during Leeds' Charity Shield triumph.

everyone to see. The League campaign got off to a fine start, with a 3-1 win over Tottenham Hotspur, but the team would win only two of their opening six fixtures; though a draw at Arsenal equalled Burnley's Division One record of 30 matches undefeated. Everton were the early pacesetters and showed their promise as potential title-challengers by defeating Leeds 3-2 at Goodison Park, ending the club's unbeaten run in the process.

We were a bit disappointed with our opening, but knew there was a long way to go. Allan and myself were still getting used to each other's style of play, but we soon clicked. I was also pleased to have scored my first goals of the season in draws against Newcastle United and Burnley.

The defeat at Goodison Park stung Leeds into action. A 2-1 victory at Sheffield Wednesday was the beginning of a run of twelve wins in sixteen matches that put the defending Champions back in the title-race. The team's performance at Hillsborough illustrated to Tom Holley of the *Yorkshire Evening Post* that there is 'no real substitute for skill'. In addition, it was clear that the partnership of Clarke and Jones was 'posing all sorts of problems'. During a tremendous run Nottingham Forest were thrashed 6-1, Ipswich 4-0 and West Ham 4-1. The victory against the

Hammers on 17 December finally overturned Everton's eight-point advantage.

We were playing some wonderful football. I remember the clash against Ipswich in particular because their 'keeper was outstanding. It's no exaggeration, we could have trebled our score, he was superb.

Although Chelsea had knocked Leeds out of the League Cup, their European Cup campaign had gone well. The first round had brought a club record 10-0 win (16-0 on aggregate) against amateurs Lyn Oslo from Norway.

The tie was clearly a mismatch, but you can only beat the teams who are put before you and the game was a particularly memorable match for me because I grabbed my first hat-trick for the club.

Mick's first goal (2-0) was a header from a Paul Reaney cross; his second (3-0) was made by Bremner's defence-splitting pass, and his hat-trick goal (8-0) came on the hour, following a pass from Bates – Jones' first-time shot hitting both posts before going in. The following morning's papers felt sorry for the Norwegians. Alan Thompson in the *Daily Express* wrote, 'it was all so easy, this merciless hammering and it could have been many more'.

A night for records. One of Mick's treble in the 10-0 annihilation of Lyn Oslo.

The second round pitted Leeds against Ferencvaros – again. Following their tight affair in the Fairs Cup, many observers believed the match could be a classic. As it transpired, Leeds dominated the home leg, winning 3-0 in muddy conditions. Leeds comfortably won the return for a 6-0 aggregate win. The victory was historic.

Frank Clough, *The Sun*: 'Mark down another 'first' for Leeds. The League Champions became the first British team to win in Hungary's Nep Stadium when they smashed aside the fallen idols of Ferencvaros. This European Cup victory was a personal triumph for Mick Jones… who carried all the hall marks – strength, courage and resolve – of a super striker.'

The players now had a break until March before they faced Standard Leige in the quarter-finals. A loss at Newcastle was soon forgotten when League leaders Everton were beaten 2-1. Acknowledged now as one of the shrewdest purchases around, Don Revie was not surprised. 'Any credit for Mick becoming an even more accomplished player should go to Syd Owen and Les Cocker. We knew he was good

Another goal against Hungary's best, this time in a Europan Cup clash.

Battling for possession with Everton's Brian Labone.

in the air and had a fantastic desire to work. We felt we could improve other aspects of his play, so we worked on his positional play and ball control and tried to get him a little fitter. Mick has been playing well all season. He was in great form against Everton, but this has been the way he has been playing week in week out. He is the best centre forward in England. Mick has strength, skill, control, and tremendous bravery. The arrival of Allan Clarke may have helped him in that the attention he receives is not always as fierce as it used to be, but I do not want to take anything away from his performances this season. He took about six months to settle down fully to our rhythm of play, which is to be expected, but after that he has never looked back. If I had to signal out one of Mick's qualities it is the fact that he never knows when to stop running, when to stop challenging, and when to stop holding off pressure.'

The win was the start of an unbeaten run when Chelsea (5-2) and West Brom (5-1) were thrashed. Leeds were also through to the FA Cup quarter-finals having beaten Swansea, Sutton and Mansfield. In addition, Mick was picked to represent the full England side again after a three-year absence.

Mick scores a late winner against Swansea Town in the FA Cup.

Goals galore against the Baggies!

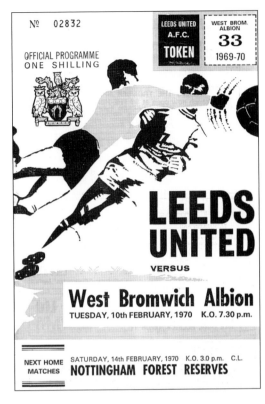

Time to relax after England duty with daughter Lindsey.

England v Holland: Banks (Leicester City), Newton (Everton), Cooper (Leeds), Peters (West Ham), J Charlton (Leeds), Hunter (Leeds), Lee (Manchester City) (sub. Mullery (Spurs) 70 min), Bell (Manchester City), Jones (Leeds) (sub. Hurst (West Ham) 75 min), R Charlton (Manchester United), Storey-Moore (Nottingham Forest).

The national press was disappointed with the goal-less result, though Mick received praise for his efforts. Alan Hubbard commented: 'Jones was given a great ovation as he trooped off and deservedly so. He had worked tirelessly, if without profit, on his international recall. He made himself a nuisance in the box, particularly in the air, and if there was to be an England goal, it seemed it would stem from his feet or head. I hope Jones gets a further opportunity to display his vigorous talents for last night his showing was the one hopeful sign that England's ills will be cured before they leave for South America.'

I won my third international cap for England against Holland. The pitch was not in the best of condition. I was obviously picked because of my club form, which delighted me, and hoped it would be the start of a sustained run in the squad, because Alf was still looking for a long-term replacement for the great Jimmy Greaves. In the Dutch side that night was the Johann Cruyff. Midway through the match he came past me like a bolt of lightning, he was so fast. He was a fantastic

Mick grabs his second in a 2-0 win over Crystal Palace.

player, and of course developed into one of the outstanding players of world football over the coming seasons.

I had quite a good match that night, but unfortunately, the score remained 0-0. During the second half, Alf brought Geoff Hurst on for me, which was disappointing because he knew what Geoff could offer, whereas I hadn't played for him for three years. I remember getting a great round of applause from the Wembley crowd, so I knew I'd played well, but I was desperately disappointed not to get picked again for the full side. One thing I regret, and I know that Allan feels the same, is that we never represented England together. I know we'd have done really well, because of the understanding we had as a partnership.

At the beginning of March anything seemed possible for Leeds United. It seemed feasible that they could defend their title and go on to win the treble. Unfortunately, the European Cup quarter-final clashes against Standard Leige were the start of serious fixture congestion, and it took its toll. When Leeds faced Celtic in the semi-final first leg at Elland Road on 1 April they'd played nine matches since the initial Liege win, including the Manchester United FA Cup trilogy. In addition, this match was the end of a four-match sequence in seven days, and the start of a three-match sequence in four days!

After their initial clash with Manchester United, Geoffrey Green of *The Times* observed: 'they say they [Leeds] relish hard work, that the expense of energy seems an eternal delight. But surely there must be a limit.' Tom Holley of the *Yorkshire Evening Post* added, 'this was the result Don Revie did NOT want'. Following the first replay with Manchester, Alan Thompson of the *Daily Express* commented, 'even defeat might have tasted sweeter to Leeds than this draw. A second replay was the last thing they want because of a demanding fixture list that is already heavily congested.'

Something had to give... and it did. With a number of the team mentally and physically fatigued, Revie was forced to rest players during the final six League fixtures. After a 3-1 defeat at home to Southampton on 28 March, Tom German of *The Times* wrote. 'If they (Leeds) lose the Championship, it is because of commitments heaped on them by the rewards of their own talents.' Two days later Revie fielded a reserve side against Derby County, signalling the end of their title challenge. The last six games would yield one win against Burnley, when Eddie Gray scored his virtuoso 'goal in a million'. Leeds ended the campaign as runners-up and focused their attention solely on the Cups.

Leading up to the semi-final clash with Celtic, Leeds finished their titanic battle against Manchester United. All three clashes were tough battles, and defences dominated. In the third game at Bolton, Billy joined Allan and myself in attack trying to get an elusive winner, and came up trumps with a great strike. There was only going to be the odd goal in it, and fortunately we just snatched it. It was magnificent

Part one of the trilogy!

Alex Stepney punches clear during the Hillsborough semi-final.

Wembley here we come!

in the dressing room afterwards. This would be my first FA Cup final and I couldn't wait. A few days later we played Celtic at Elland Road. They caught us out with a sloppy goal from our part, but they were the better side on the night.'

A visitor at the game was Liverpool boss Bill Shankly, who had nothing but sympathy for the home side with the cup final coming up. 'Chelsea could win the FA Cup final… but they are not in the same class as Leeds United… Everton have won the League Championship while the best team this country has seen for a long time is in a position where it might win nothing… this has been a vicious season for Leeds. The whole world has come down on them. Celtic were healthy and strong, Leeds were not… They had faced too many injuries and too many games.' As for the cup final, Shankly added, 'if Leeds are beaten it will complete a tragic season for them'.

The players rested for a week and it showed in their performance at Wembley, despite playing on a pitch in terrible condition.

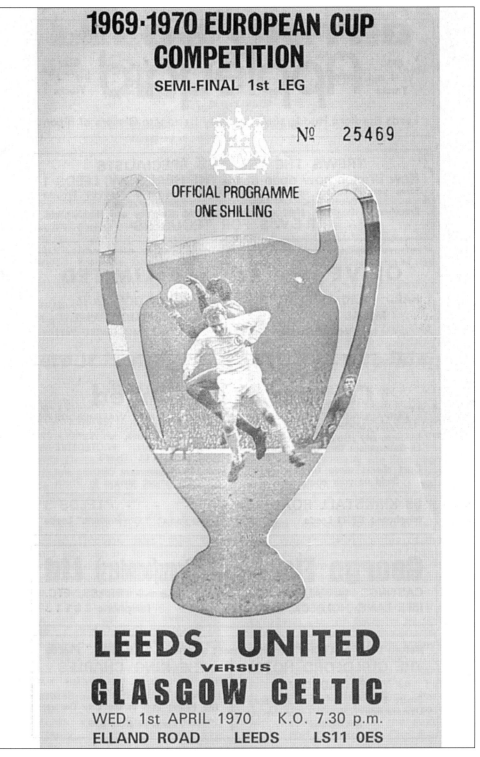

Another semi-final, this time in the European Cup.

Mick goes close, but Celtic pinched a win.

Leeds United, 1970 FA Cup final squad. From left to right, back row: Reaney, Sprake, Harvey, Cooper. Middle row: Bremner, Hunter, Charlton, Madeley, Yorath. Front row: Gray, Lorimer, Giles, Bates, Clarke, Jones, Hibbitt, Belfitt.

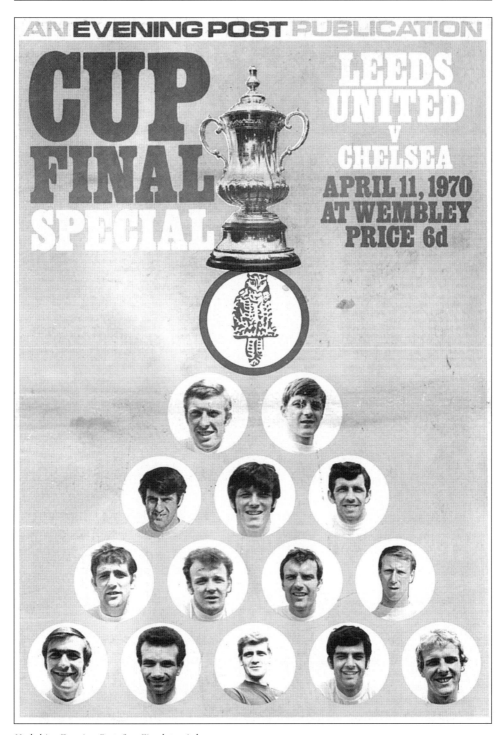

Yorkshire Evening Post Cup Final special.

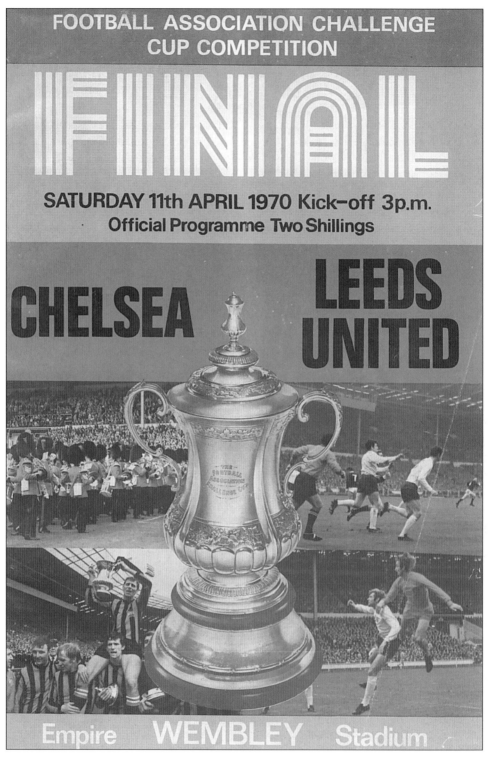

Mick's first FA Cup final.

Chelsea v Leeds United, 1970 FA Cup final:

Chelsea: Bonetti, Webb, McCreadie, Hollins, Dempsey, Harris (captain), Baldwin, Houseman, Osgood, Hutchison, Cooke; sub: Hinton.

Leeds United: Sprake, Madeley, Cooper, Bremner (captain), Charlton, Hunter, Lorimer, Clarke, Jones, Giles, Gray; sub: Bates.

The match ended in a 2-2 draw resulting in a replay for the first time in fifty-eight years. Following a pulsating encounter Geoffrey Green wrote, 'it was not a classic but an epic... the finest final seen at Wembley since the war... it had everything from A to Z'.

Barry Foster, *Yorkshire Post*, added: 'After all their efforts this season it will be something of an injustice if Leeds United finish empty-handed, yet Leeds still have to produce the knock-out blow... Leeds set Wembley alight with one of their extra special displays... They used the wide-open spaces of Wembley with great control and accuracy despite sand-covered stretches, which played havoc with the bounce, and speed of the ball.'

Don Revie was proud of his players and delighted that they had 'showed everybody we can still play'. He had 'never seen them play better' and found it amazing where the players kept finding their energy from. 'I don't think we'll hear any more about unattractive Leeds after today!'

Don Revie and Dave Sexton lead their teams out at Wembley.

The match may have gone down as one of the greatest of all-time but it is one Mick Jones recalls with mixed feelings.

As a young boy it was one of my dreams to play at Wembley in an FA Cup final, and as a player it was one of my great ambitions. When we arrived at the stadium and went on the pitch, I could not believe it. They'd just had the Horse of the Year Show and the pitch was in a terrible state; you sank a few inches, it was so heavy. It was not the Wembley you normally saw on television with a lovely playing surface, however it was the same for both sides. With it being so muddy we took a salt tablet to avoid cramp. I didn't like them, but it was a necessity that day.

It was a cracking game, one of the best finals ever. Big Jack gave us the lead when his header from a corner stuck in the mud and bobbled over the line, before Gary made a terrible blunder just before half-time from Houseman's speculative shot. At the time I thought… not again… not in such a crucial game. It didn't look a hard save; he just had to get his body behind it. It was a bad misjudgement. Jack gave him a real rollicking! At half time we didn't discuss it; Gary knew how bad his mistake was, and we all knew that as a 'keeper his errors always stood out more than ours.

Leeds on the attack during a Wembley thriller.

Eight minutes remaining and Mick gives Leeds a 2-1 lead.

We still thought we'd win though. Eddie Gray was having a magnificent game and giving David Webb a roasting on the left-hand side. We really took control in the second half and hit the woodwork a number of times, then with about eight minutes to go I remember Billy knocking a ball forward to Johnny Giles who whipped it in from the right hand side. Allan headed it against a post and it came towards me. Because of the heavy pitch just before I hit the ball it bobbled up and I caught it spot on. The ball fitted perfectly in the corner. I thought 'that's it... we've won'. As I turned around Don Revie signalled that there were only eight minutes to go.

Of course, it's never over, but with the way both defences had played I couldn't see another goal being scored. Unfortunately, we gave away an unnecessary free kick near our penalty area. They equalised through Hutchison and the match went into extra-time. I was the first to go down with cramp; even Norman went down which shows how bad it was. By the end both teams were happy to settle for a replay, but we should have won in the second half when we were so much on top. However, you must give Chelsea credit because they hung in the game. In the dressing room after we could not believe we hadn't won, although we obviously thought we could go to Old Trafford and win because we'd been the better side.

Leeds may have been held 2-2, but the boys are still in fine voice, along with Don Revie's daughter Kim.

From Wembley Leeds flew to Scotland for a return encounter with Celtic.

I've never known an atmosphere like it, 136,500 fans packed into the stadium; it was electric. Billy scored a magnificent goal to level the tie on aggregate. Bertie Auld caught me with a terrible challenge in a fifty-fifty ball. If I'd not been wearing shin pads, he'd have broken my leg. I was carried off. Gary got injured and was replaced by David Harvey in goal. They scored twice to win 3-1 on aggregate, but there was nothing to be ashamed of because they were a great side. Their star was Jimmy Johnstone who gave Terry Cooper a torrid time, which was rare because Terry was arguably the best around in his position. Where we lost the tie was at Elland Road, when we didn't do ourselves justice.

After a season that promised so much only the FA Cup remained, there would be two weeks to prepare.

All of Scotland wanted to see this 'Battle of Britain' clash.

FA CUP FINAL REPLAY
OLD TRAFFORD · MANCHESTER

2/-

Chelsea

Leeds
U N I T E D

April 29th 1970 Kick Off 7·30pm
OFFICIAL PROGRAMME
Published by Manchester United Football Club

The FA Cup final, part two.

Chelsea v Leeds United, 1970 FA Cup final replay:

Chelsea: Bonetti, Webb, McCreadie, Hollins, Dempsey, Harris (captain), Baldwin, Houseman, Osgood, Hutchison, Cooke; sub: Hinton.
Leeds United: Sprake, Madeley, Cooper, Bremner (captain), Charlton, Hunter, Lorimer, Clarke, Jones, Giles, Gray; sub: Bates.

Leeds were refreshed but Chelsea had also regrouped and altered their formation. Ron Harris marked Eddie Gray, not David Webb. In a game summed up by Geoffrey Green as 'one with vicious tackling – Boadicea might have been on parade', Mick gave Leeds a first half lead but Chelsea proved resilient again when Osgood equalised near the end. In a cruel twist, Webb scored the extra-time winner. Don Revie was naturally choked, but vowed to 'start again next season.'

One reporter was so moved he wrote next day, 'in any other walk of life, you could get twenty years for robbery. In football, if you're Chelsea, you rob Leeds of their rightful possession of the FA Cup. Just how they did it is beyond my comprehension'.

We just couldn't believe it; we were so disappointed we went straight back to the dressing rooms forgetting to collect our medals. Obviously I was pleased with my goal, running about forty yards before smacking it in, but they came back. Over the two games I thought we deserved to win but you must give Chelsea credit, because they kept battling away.

Naturally, we were distraught. We went to the players' lounge before we set off back to Leeds. I recall talking to Peter Osgood after the game, although they'd beaten us he felt we were the best British team there had been. That was tremendous coming from another professional footballer. We learned a lot that season, even though we came out with nothing.

Towards the end of the season we had no alternative but to go for everything we were involved in, so you had to do your best. In any case, it's very difficult to just target the

League, FA Cup or European Cup. It wasn't that we were physically tired, even though we had to play so many games in a short period, but we were mentally tired.

With all the matches, training consisted of loosening exercises, sprints, some ball-work and a five-a-side match. Of course, we all carried the odd injury, but that was part and parcel of the game. It had been a superb season however, even though it ended so disappointingly, after all, how many players get the chance of going for the treble.

Mick was also delighted with how his partnership with Allan Clarke had developed.

John Dempsey makes life awkward, with David Webb in support.

Once again, Mick gives Leeds the lead – but it wasn't to be.

With the arrival of Allan we now had a really dangerous attack. Allan was the final piece of the team. Don always told me I was doing an excellent job, but in Allan he spotted something different and we both gained when we partnered each other. I'd played against him during his days at Fulham and Leicester City, and with him in the England under-23s. We soon became friends off the field, and it's a friendship that has lasted ever since.

Allan had a tag that he could be a problem-player, which you couldn't be at Leeds, or you would soon know about it, but in fairness from his first day at the club, he was nothing like the press had made out. On his arrival, he found a group of players who were as ambitious as he was and he settled immediately. It took us a while to get a good understanding, but once it had developed, we never once collided. One of the major reasons it worked was because we were two completely different types of players. We had a fantastic season, finishing joint-top scorers with 26 goals apiece. The campaign was my most prolific as a goal scorer for Leeds. Though I was really disappointed we'd failed to win any silverware, I was soon looking ahead to the new season.

8

COLCHESTER, TINKLER AND WATERLOGGED PITCHES
1970/71

When Leeds returned for pre-season training, the disappointments of the previous campaign were soon forgotten.

I had a good rest and enjoyed watching the World Cup finals in Mexico during the summer. I'd liked to have been a part of the England squad, but missed out when the squad was cut to twenty-eight. When we returned there was no moping about. We simply got on with it determined to win more trophies, and did we train hard; there was no choice though because of all the matches we knew we'd be playing.

I loved the dressing room banter; I got changed next to Billy. There was a lot of mickey taking, but it was all harmless fun – and if you took it the wrong way you were in trouble. I took the brunt of the stick. The three main culprits were Billy, Gilsey and Clarkie. When you walked in on a morning, they'd look you up and down. If you had a bit of a coloured tie on, or your shirt was an odd colour, you certainly knew it!

Training-wise, it was brilliant. We did a lot of ball-work and, for the five-a-side games, we often played Scotland against England. Anyone watching at Fullerton Park would have thought it was an FA Cup final; the commitment was unbelievable. At the end of a match we used to vote who was the best player. The winner would count up the votes for the worst player before announcing who would have to wear a yellow jersey the next day. Nobody wanted this 'honour' because you got incredible stick. You certainly played your heart out next day! It was all part of the competitive environment instilled by Don... and it worked.

Leeds began the season in scintillating fashion, winning their opening five fixtures before a stalemate against Arsenal ended their fine start. The team's win on the opening day was particularly special for Mick because he scored his 100th League goal – a header Alan Thompson in the *Daily Express* described as one that would 'live in the memory for ever'. Speaking to the *Sunday Express*, Manchester's manager Wilf

Leeds United, 1970/71. From left to right, back row: Galvin, Yorath, Harvey, Jones, Sprake, Charlton, Clarke, Hunter, Gray, Madeley. Front row: Belfitt, Reaney, Lorimer, Giles, Bremner, Cooper, Bates, Hibbitt.

McGuiness lamented, 'goals like that shouldn't be allowed – not on the first day of the season… when he headed it from that position I couldn't believe it, he'll probably never score another like that all his career'.

Consistent performances kept Leeds at the forefront, despite two more Sprake blunders, which cost vital goals.

Unfortunately, Gary made occasional mistakes, which was down to concentration. Before games, Don would point to his head and emphasise that he had to concentrate because often he'd only have the odd shot to save. When Gary was busy he was brilliant, but when he wasn't his concentration lapsed.

During the season, when we played Crystal Palace he let in a last-minute equaliser, but his most stunning mistake was in a clash against Liverpool. Playing at Anfield was always a tough match. In one particular game Gary had the ball in his hands at the eighteen-yard box. It looked like he was going to throw the ball out to Terry Cooper; however, halfway through his throw he lost control and threw the ball into the net. I'd never seen a goal like it; I could not believe it! Thousands of hands went up in the Kop, as one they started singing the song 'Careless Hands', which was pretty cruel.

A defeat against Tottenham in the opening game of the New Year was (incredibly) only the second of Leeds' League campaign. Whilst going strong in the League, the players were also making steady progress in the FA Cup. Mick scored his second hat-trick for Leeds in a fourth round win against Swindon, which set up a fifth round clash against a Fourth Division side… Colchester United. In one of the greatest upsets of all-time the underdogs beat Don Revie's mighty team.

Barry Foster for the *Yorkshire Post* commented: 'A side as superstitious as Leeds might have known something extraordinary was on the cards on the 13th of the month but to be the giant in the biggest giant-killing act since Jack and the Beanstalk was a terrible blow to take.'

The match at Colchester is one cup tie I'll never forget but for all the wrong reasons. Even today, people never stop reminding me about that game, along with the one against Sunderland in '73. There were no excuses really; the better team won, simple

Easy does it… Les Cocker runs the players through their paces.

Mick gets the better of Arsenal's John Roberts at Highbury.

Celebration time after an FA Cup hat-trick against Swindon Town.

The biggest shock of all – Colchester 3 Leeds 2.

as that. They scored three goals through some bad defensive errors, which was most unlike us. We pulled it back to 3-2, but it was too late to get back into the game. Sometimes you get these freak results, but the pitch was horrendous. It was so bumpy and bouncy, which hindered our style of play, and brought us to their level. No complaints though, it was a shock result – but that's what the FA Cup is all about.

Leeds bounced back immediately with consecutive wins over Wolves, Ipswich Town, Coventry City and Derby County. They were now in a position whereby, with eight games remaining, they held a six-point lead over their nearest challengers Arsenal, who had two games in hand.

Following a 4-0 win at Burnley at the beginning of April, all was well in the Leeds camp. However, draws against Newcastle and Huddersfield Town meant the players faced a crunch match at home to West Brom. The Midlanders arrived at Elland Road without an away win in sixteen months. *Match of the Day* was analysing key moments from a game with slow motion replays and televised the match that evening. Ray Tinkler refereed the match.

Ranked among the most infamous of games in the club's history, the media explosion following West Brom's 2-1 win was unbelievable. Don Revie went on television; everybody was talking about the game – and that goal! Revie commented bitterly after

Derby's Colin Boulton saves his team – but he couldn't prevent Lorimer's winner.

Mick soars above Huddersfield's Dennis Clarke, but Roy Ellam (a future Leeds player) clears the ball.

the game that 'nine months hard work was sent down the drain by a referee's decision'. As for Mr Tinkler, he was adamant that the player involved in the incident, Colin Suggett, 'was not interfering with play... therefore there was no need to whistle'. Tinkler had few supporters and had to be escorted from the pitch by police.

It looked possible that we would win the title again, but after leading throughout the campaign, Arsenal hit a rich vein of form and began closing on us. Our penultimate home game was against West Brom. We needed a win to stay in pole position. Although we went a goal down, I scored with a header, but for some reason the referee Ray Tinkler ruled that an infringement had taken place. None of us could believe it. Within a couple of minutes, they scored a goal that was definitely offside. How the referee allowed it, I will never know.

Tony Brown intercepted a pass by Norman Hunter and broke across the halfway line. The linesman immediately raised his flag for offside because Colin Suggett was returning from a previous attack, he was clearly offside. Everyone stopped, but Tinkler waved play on. Brown carried the ball forward before squaring it to Jeff Astle, who side-footed the ball in.

Goal ... no it's not! Ray Tinkler rules out Mick's effort against West Brom for offside.

None of us could believe the goal had been given, but the referee was adamant; the goal stood. The crowd was also incensed and a number of them raced onto the pitch; they were so frustrated. What riled them so much was that after my goal was unluckily chalked off, a blatant offside goal was given. I managed to stop one person as he raced towards the referee, he was so angry. If he'd reached him, I hate to think what he'd have done.

I'm convinced that if my goal had stood we'd have gone on to win the game, but the decision knocked us back. We managed to score a consolation goal, but it was too late. We won our last three games, but lost the title to Arsenal by a point. Every team has ups and downs during a season, but that match was the key game. Tickler's decision ultimately cost us the Championship.

Leeds had one chance left to avoid a repeat of the previous season and win some silverware – the Fairs Cup. Leeds started the campaign well, easily overcoming Sarpsbourg 6-0 on aggregate, before squeezing past Dynamo Dresden on the away goals rule. Following an emphatic 9-2 aggregate win over Sparta Prague, Leeds experienced another tight tie when they just beat the crack Portuguese side Vitoria Setubal 3-2 on aggregate. In the semi-finals Leeds faced their old enemies Liverpool.

Leeds fans invade the pitch following West Brom's controversial 'offside goal'.

The Wizard comic's tribute to Mick Jones (May 1971).

Don gambled by bringing Billy back for the first leg at Anfield after a long lay-off and it paid off because he grabbed a priceless goal for us. It was an incredibly tense affair, but we just held on. The second leg was just as difficult, both Allan and myself went off injured so Joe Jordan had to play the lone striker and did a great job. We drew 0-0 to book ourselves a place in the final once again, which was a tremendous relief, because at the time the title was slipping away.

Leeds had reached their third Fairs Cup final in five years, a fantastic achievement. Following the disappointment of the previous campaign when they ended the season with nothing, Revie was determined his players would finish the season with a trophy, despite having to face the mighty Juventus. Talking with reporters before the game Revie promised his team would be 'going harder over the next two matches than they have ever done in the ten years I have been in charge'.

Before the opening game in Turin, Italian papers predicted an easy win for Juventus, but after missing out in the League, we were fired up. I had never seen us as sharp so far into a season. Our wives came over with us for the final, but from the moment we arrived it poured down. The first leg was in doubt right up the last minute. Rain had fallen for days prior to the match, forcing UEFA to plan for the game not taking place if the adverse conditions continued. Eventually the match did go ahead.

Juventus had a tremendous side, which included the likes of Bettaga, Capello, Anastasi and Causio, but they knew they'd be in for a game because we had a great reputation in Europe. The conditions for the match were appalling. Throughout the day it had rained. When we kicked off the rain was torrential, within minutes there was a storm. The match shouldn't have started, you couldn't control the ball properly, judge passes or lay the ball off with confidence; it was a lottery, which was such a shame because there was fantastic talent on the pitch.

Early in the second half, the referee finally abandoned the game, which we were disappointed about because the score was 0-0, and it looked likely that it would stay that way. In addition, Eddie Gray picked up an injury in the slippery conditions, which meant he'd miss both legs of the final. We went back to the hotel. The storm eventually blew over and we replayed the game a couple of days later.

Juventus v Leeds United, 1971 Fairs Cup final first leg:

Juventus: Piloni, Spinosi, Marchetti, Furino, Morino, Salvadore, Haller, Causio, Anastasi, Capello, Bettaga; sub: Novellini.
Leeds United: Sprake, Reaney, Cooper, Bremner (captain), Charlton, Hunter, Lorimer, Clarke, Jones, Giles, Madeley; sub: Bates.

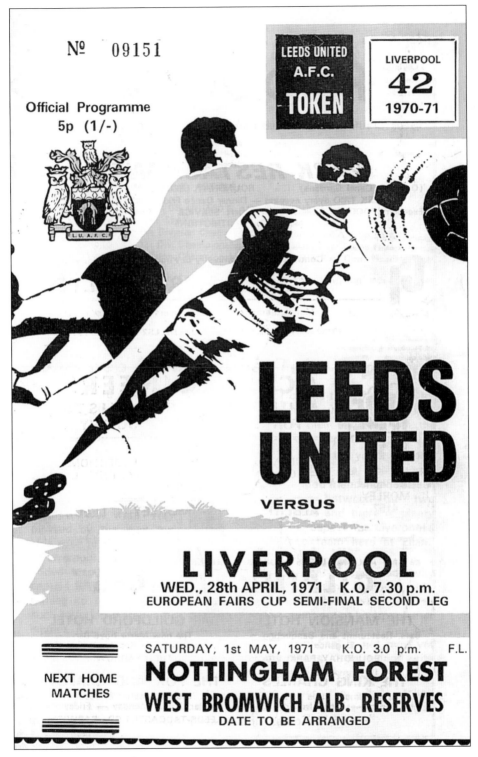

A classic against Liverpool in Europe.

Torrential rain during the ill-fated Fairs Cup final first leg.

Mick pressurises Piloni and Salvadore in a classic 2-2 draw in Turin.

Leeds United's performance at the Stadio Comunale was one of the 'finest displays of courage, enlightened football and determination' Barry Foster of the *Yorkshire Post* had witnessed. In a sensational game, full of entertaining football, Leeds twice came from behind to cancel out superb goals from the Juventus millionaires forward line. At times playing against a blanket defence, they succeeded in masterly fashion.

Speed captures the 'waterlogged pitch' incident in his weekly Yorkshire Evening Post cartoon.

Left: Yorkshire Evening Post Fairs Cup final special. Right: How many millions would these players be worth now?

We knew it was going to be tough and they were a class act, but we matched them and scored two priceless away goals through Paul Madeley and Mick Bates to draw 2-2, which was a fantastic result. However, we knew the return would not be a formality but we were confident we could win.

Leeds United v Juventus, 1971 Fairs Cup final second leg:

Leeds United: Sprake, Reaney, Cooper, Bremner (captain), Charlton, Hunter, Lorimer, Clarke, Jones, Giles, Madeley; sub: Bates.
Juventus: Tancredi, Spinosi, Marchetti, Furino, Morino, Salvadore, Haller, Causio, Anastasi, Capello, Bettaga; sub: Novellini.

The second leg was a great game because Juventus knew a draw would not be enough, so they were more attack-minded than they would normally have been. Allan gave us an early lead, which proved crucial. Although they equalised, we were so solid at the back; I just couldn't see them scoring again. Terry Cooper was superb throughout the match and gave them a lot of problems down the left flank. Afterwards the feeling was one of relief; it was terrific to end the season on a high again.

On many occasions people have told me that we never won the trophies we should have, which in some ways is true, but we were always in the mix for honours. If you look at our era, a number of teams got to semi-finals and finals of tournaments and fell at the last stage; we weren't the only ones. However, for consistency no one could match us. People used to say we should just target the FA Cup; it's simply not possible. Our nature was to go for the lot and see what transpired.

Throughout a season we were always involved in big games. From the day I joined Leeds every team we played against raised their game, it was their match of the season, but we got used to it. Supporters around the country feared us; our opponents were no different, which says a lot about what we achieved. We were all household names; everyone knew our side. Even today, although other teams like Arsenal, Everton, Liverpool, Manchester City and Manchester United all had outstanding players, whenever I meet fans they can all reel off our entire team: Sprake, Reaney, Cooper, Bremner, Charlton, Hunter... whereas quite often they only remember some of the stars from other teams.

Throughout the campaign I struggled for goals. I'd started reasonably well, but for some reason, after October I had a really lean spell. When this occurs as a recognised

Piloni just gets to the ball first in the second leg clash at Elland Road.

A close shave against Juventus.

goalscorer, you begin to lose confidence. No matter what I tried, the goals dried up. I went to see Don Revie and suggested he left me out of the side, but he refused.

When you're scoring, you can't wait to get out onto the park, but I was having a hard time. It happens to every striker, but Don told me I was doing a marvellous job, we were getting results and he had every confidence in me. He knew the goals would come back. He even said, if I didn't score all season he'd still play me because I brought more to the team than just goals, which meant a lot to me.

Celebration time after the Fairs Cup triumph.

Eventually I broke the spell at Southampton; the relief was incredible. To cap a memorable day it was my birthday! Don never said anything, but he had a wry smile on his face. From then on, I was fine. In some ways, I was better off than some strikers because supporters knew I was giving my all so they were always very encouraging, but I was glad to break the lean spell. Fortunately, it was the only time at Leeds when I had this problem, but I've never forgotten how Don supported me. I shouldn't have been surprised though, because Don's man-management skills were superb.

The atmosphere at Elland Road was fantastic, and credit for that must go to Don Revie, who we all thought the world of. As a man-manager, he was terrific; he always

Mick takes on Jimmy Gabriel at The Dell. Two goals in this game ended his scoring drought.

got the best out of us. He thought of everything, even if it meant 'conning' you on the odd occasion! Once I was feeling a little under the weather. I had flu and was in bed. I told Glenis to phone the ground and tell them I wouldn't be in for a couple of days because I didn't want to spread the virus. Within an hour, there was a knock at the door. Don had sent flowers and a big basket of fruit with a note 'get well soon, get back as quick as possible'. I was back next day!

Nothing was too much trouble for Don, who believed that everyone at the club mattered. Whenever we got to a cup final tickets were like gold dust. During the build up one year, a window cleaner at the club was going through his usual routine when Don called him over. He thought he was in trouble, but all Don wanted to know was whether he wanted to go to the cup final with his family. He could not believe that Don had gone out of his way for him, but that's what he was like. Everybody behind the scenes was important, the laundry ladies, stewards, the cleaners. We were all one family.

We had a terrific squad at Leeds; a number of internationals didn't play each week, which says an awful lot about the talent Don Revie developed. Very few asked to leave, which demonstrated Don's man-management skills. However, one thing I could never understand was his superstitious nature. A number of players had the odd superstition; what order they put their strip on, or the order they lined up when we went out (Jack always liked coming out last, as Allan did), but Don had a number of them. Once he had gypsies down at Elland Road to remove a curse, and on another occasion, he went barmy when someone left a boot on a table in the dressing room before a game. However, his most famous superstition was his 'lucky blue suit', which he wore to every match.

Before one particular game, Don was giving us his pre-match team talk after we had finished our ritual light lunch. Suddenly, he dropped his notes on the floor. As he bent down to retrieve them, his trousers split. His face had panic written all over it. He changed into a pair of tracksuit bottoms and made a quick phone call to get his trousers repaired. We went down to the ground, about 2.30 p.m. his trousers had not arrived back; he was not happy. A couple of minutes before we were due to go out someone rushed in to the dressing room with his trousers. Immediately he relaxed, the relief on his face was incredible. We won the match! As a manager, he was fantastic and was respected by everyone, but it never made sense to me why he was so superstitious. That said, his record is unrivalled at Leeds United.

9
UP FOR THE CUP
1971/72

Before a ball had been kicked in the 1971/72 campaign, the club had to reflect on the fallout of the pitch invasion during the clash against West Brom. Whilst there was nationwide agreement that Tinkler's decision was unjust, football's governing body banned Leeds from playing their first three home games at Elland Road.

*Leeds United squad 1971/72. From left to right, **back row**: Belfitt, Hunter, Sprake, Harvey, Jordan, Yorath. Middle row: Faulkner, Galvin, Jones, Madeley, Clarke, Charlton. Front row: Reaney, Bates, Lorimer, Giles, Bremner, Davey, Cooper.*

Disadvantaged from the beginning, Leeds began the season poorly, losing as many League games by mid-November as in the whole of the previous campaign. Surprisingly, they had also been knocked out of the UEFA Cup at the first stage. It didn't help matters that the club's two main strikers were both injured, indeed their first League game together during the campaign was against Manchester City in October: both scored in a 3-0 win.

As a pair they were becoming irreplaceable. 'You can put deputies in some positions without affecting the impetus of the side, but it just can't be done up front,' Revie told reporters. 'Neither was really fit, Jones hadn't trained for seven weeks and Clarke four weeks, but we needed their experience. On top of that they really wanted to play.'

After overcoming an injury when I first joined Leeds, this was the first period I had at the club when I was out for a sustained period of time. I'd picked up the injury in a pre-season friendly and it was frustrating. We all played with niggling injuries at times, but sometimes only rest cures a problem. Seeing the lads struggle, by our standards, was not enjoyable. I remember the City clash, because we had gone through an indifferent spell and I was desperate to play. We won but I was sidelined for a further month and Allan was also soon out injured again.

Both returned following a defeat at Southampton in late November. This time there would be no reactions. Leeds soon climbed the table. After a comfortable 2-0 win at Nottingham Forest, an impressed Matt Gillies (Forest's manager) told the *Express* that everything was back to normal at Leeds United. 'Make no mistake, Leeds are still the finest team in the country. They may have had their troubles early in the season but they are now showing real poise and assurance. They'll take some stopping.'

By Christmas, Leeds were five points adrift from the top. Following a two-goal victory at Anfield on New Year's Day they were back in the pack with a fully-fit squad. The win at Liverpool was the turning point of the season, and not just because they had inflicted the first home defeat in 35 matches on their great rivals, but because it summed up the quality of their performances in recent weeks.

'Clarke and Jones Leave Kop Speechless' headlined the *Yorkshire Post*. Barry Foster, like many of his colleagues, was impressed. 'Leeds United are playing their most accomplished football since they became a major power in the game. With Clarke and Jones in goal-scoring mood, Leeds will take some stopping. Seldom has a team started the New Year so right on the field.'

I hadn't trained for weeks so it took me a while to get match-fit, but playing again was fantastic. Our confidence was sky high after the 2-0 win Anfield. We really hit form and went on a superb run.

N⁰ 26313

LEEDS UNITED A.F.C. TOKEN

MANCHESTER UNITED 22 1971-72

Official Programme 5p

LEEDS UNITED
versus MANCHESTER UNITED

Saturday, 19th February, 1972   Kick-off 3 p.m.   at ELLAND ROAD

Allan Clarke beats the Liverpool defence and finally the goalkeeper to put home his first goal.
Photo by Jack Hickes, Leeds

Leeds United
Colours :
WHITE SHIRTS, WHITE SHORTS

1. GARY SPRAKE
2. PAUL REANEY
3. TERRY COOPER
4. BILLY BREMNER
5. JACK CHARLTON
6. NORMAN HUNTER
7. PETER LORIMER
8. ALLAN CLARKE
9. PAUL MADELEY
10. JOHNNY GILES
11. EDDIE GRAY

Sub.

Manchester Utd
Colours :
RED SHIRTS, WHITE SHORTS

1. ALEX STEPNEY
2. TOMMY O'NEIL
3. FRANCIS BURNS
4. ALAN GOWLING
5. STEVE JAMES
6. DAVID SADLER
7. WILLIE MORGAN
8. BRIAN KIDD
9. BOBBY CHARLTON
10. DENIS LAW
11. GEORGE BEST

Sub.

Referee : Mr. N. C. BURTENSHAW, Great Yarmouth
Linesmen : Mr. A. W. GREY, Gorleston-on-Sea (Red Flag)
Mr. T. FARLEY, Newton Aycliffe, Co. Durham (Yellow Flag)

It doesn't get much better… 5-1!

Mick scores his second against Manchester United.

The coming weeks would produce scintillating football from Leeds, in particular the destruction of Manchester United 5-1 and Southampton 7-0. The clash against Manchester United brought Mick Jones his third hat-trick for the club with goals after 47, 58 and 64 minutes. His first goal was a result of following up an Eddie Gray shot and knocking in the rebound, the second came from a fine cross from his skipper Billy Bremner and his hat-trick goal resulted when he diverted a Peter Lorimer shot home. The result brought rave reviews.

Tom Holley, *Yorkshire Evening Post*: 'Rampant Leeds completed their "double double" over the Manchester clubs, and if you think the Old Trafford men were "tanned" you are dead right. It should have been 10-1.'

Brian Glanville, *Sunday Times*: 'The spectacle was almost that of the matador toying with a weary bull, the delighted roars of the crowd at each new piece of virtuosity the equivalent of the "Oles" of the bullring.'

Ronald Crowther, *Daily Mail*: 'Leeds, as we saw in this superb display of selfless, non-stop running, are essentially a team without any exhibitionist or would-be virtuoso. They had eleven stars all clinically efficient in this demolition of their arch-rivals from Manchester.'

After the game, Jones spoke to reporters.

I can't recall when we've played better, everything went right and chances just seemed to drop at my feet. Although I've missed a lot of matches this season because of injury, my job is to score, but my role involves more than that. I'm expected to stir things up, score if the chances come, but firstly create things for other players. Supporters sometimes lose sight of this, but players, especially Allan Clarke, never do, and the boss appreciates what I do and that's what matters most.

Looking back, Mick recalls:

We were really beginning to hit our peak. The clash with Manchester United for me was especially memorable because I scored a hat-trick. All goals are special, but a treble in such a high profile game was particularly pleasing.

Leeds next game against Southampton made neutrals gasp at *Match of the Day's* televised coverage. The team attracted acclaim as much for their sustained game of keep ball when the match was comprehensively won, as for the quality of football. After the match an ecstatic Don Revie said, 'I'm not saying anything. I've said it all before. You say it.' Reporters did!

Take that!... Mick grabs his third.

Hat-trick hero!

Nᵒ 19256

LEEDS UNITED A.F.C. TOKEN

SOUTHAMPTON 23 1971-72

Official Programme 5p

LEEDS UNITED

versus SOUTHAMPTON

Saturday, 4th March, 1972   Kick-off 3 p.m.   at ELLAND ROAD

Photo by Jack Hickes, Leeds

Leeds United

Colours :
WHITE SHIRTS, WHITE SHORTS

1. GARY SPRAKE
2. PAUL MADELEY
3. TERRY COOPER
4. BILLY BREMNER
5. JACK CHARLTON
6. NORMAN HUNTER
7. PETER LORIMER
8. ALLAN CLARKE
9. MICK JONES
10. JOHNNY GILES
11. EDDIE GRAY

Sub.

Southampton

Colours :
RED & WHITE SHIRTS, BLACK SHORTS

1. ERIC MARTIN
2. BOB McCARTHY
3. ROGER FRY
4. JIM STEELE
5. JIMMY GABRIEL
6. TONY BYRNE
7. TERRY PAINE
8. MIKE CHANNON
9. RON DAVIES
10. GERRY O'BRIEN
11. BOBBY STOKES

Sub.

Referee : Mr. D. CORBETT, Wolverhampton
Linesmen : Mr. A. GORTON, Macclesfield (Red Flag)
Mr. P. BIRCHALL, Bolton (Yellow Flag)

Ole! Ole!

160

The *Sunday Express* reporter was exultant in his praise. 'Leeds United unveiled a treasure trove of memorable football riches... Southampton belonged to another league; Leeds to another world.'

Mike Casey, *Yorkshire Evening Post*: 'Skill, individual flair, teamwork, non-stop effort and devastating marksmanship... Don Revie's championship claimants had all these virtues in abundance.'

As for the vanquished Saints players, when interviewed after the game, defender Jimmy Gabriel said, 'Leeds have just about reached perfection...They are the nearest thing to footballing utopia. They used to be hard, niggling and unpopular, but they've come through all the phases and developed into a truly wonderful side. They're telepathic. You don't hear their players shout, they seem to know just where there mates are... Leeds have now reached the stage where they could destroy any side'. Southampton's manager, Ted Bates added: 'When you see a team play like they did you must rate them as one of the finest in the world'.

Against Southampton, when we were seven up the lads in midfield were knocking the ball about. The style of the performance was superb. People often think that it's only the midfielders who have the tricks and skills, but, during the latter stages of the game,

Mick scores number seven in the annihilation of Southampton.

Another goal, this time against Arsenal in a 3-0 win.

all the players joined in to knock the ball about. I was stood at the front and Big Jack was at the back, we were both dreading the ball coming towards us in case we lost it! The crowd loved it, they were chanting 'ole…ole'; it was exhibition stuff and fabulous to be part of. It may have looked easy but it wasn't. It takes a lot of skill, belief and confidence to perform like that.

Everyone stills talks about our victories over Manchester United and Southampton; however, a few weeks later we hammered Arsenal 3-0 and Nottingham Forest 6-1. We were playing some exceptional football.

After a difficult start to the campaign, it had been a remarkable turnaround, and the team was receiving national acclaim – a point acknowledged by Don Revie in an interview with John Sadler. 'When we came into the First Division eight years ago they slung a terrible cruel tag around our necks. They called us the dirtiest team in the land; that was a lousy label to give a team of youngsters. We were booed on every ground, booked for almost every hard tackle. It's only now that we've managed to live it down. Now they are accepting us a great team.'

'I would like the current team to be remembered as ambassadors of football. I'm sure in years to come they will talk about us as one of the truly great football sides of world football. We are reaching the stage where we don't need to be compared to anyone. We are who we are – Leeds United. We've learned to have absolute belief in our ability. We believe in ourselves and at last other people seem to believe in us.'

Even though Leeds slipped up during the Easter fixtures they were right back in the title race, and through to the semi-finals of the FA Cup. Leeds charge to the last four of the FA Cup had been impressive. The run began with a straightforward 4-1 win over Bristol Rovers in the third round. The players' reward was a trip to Anfield to face Liverpool.

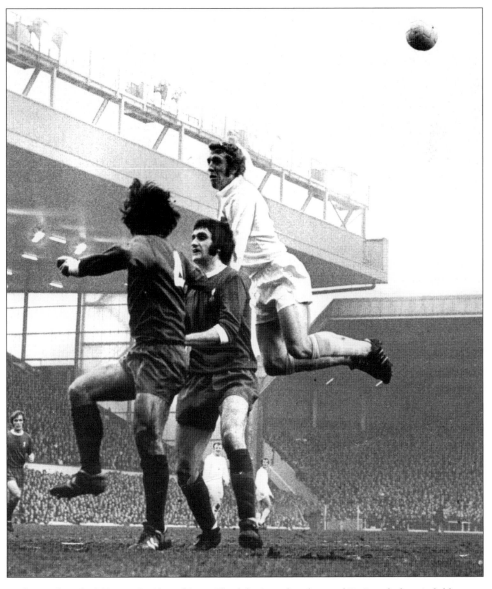

Mick gets above both Tommy Smith and Larry Lloyd during a fourth round FA Cup clash at Anfield.

We knew it would be tight, and it was. They had the best chances but we ground out a tremendous result. Thousands were locked out of the replay, which was a pity, because it was a superb game. Allan came up trumps with a couple of great goals. With Liverpool out we fancied our chances.

John Giles scored a brace of goals at Cardiff in the fifth round. Michael Boon of the *Sunday Express* summed up the team's fifth round triumph: 'smooth as cream… Leeds are as rich in talent as any club side in the world'. Leeds now faced Tottenham in the quarter-finals. The Londoners played well, but Leeds were in imperious form, coming from a goal behind to win 2-1. It could have been far worse, but Pat Jennings made a number of world class saves and kept the score respectable.

Brian James of the *Sunday Times* thought the game had 'as many moments of near perfection as football can get'. As for Terry Brindle of the *Yorkshire Post*, he believed that Leeds 'should be a short-price for the Boat Race, the Grand National and the British Grand Prix (on foot), let alone the Cup!' Don Warters at the *Yorkshire Evening Post* was in no doubt where Leeds was heading. 'The twin towers of Wembley are beckoning and Leeds United are answering them loud and clear.'

Tottenham's Pat Jennings is helpless as his defenders clear off the line in a sensational quarter-final.

Fans vie for a prize possession – Mick's stocking tabs.

The game was also notable for being the first when Leeds went through a five-minute warm-up routine, wearing individual track suits – each bearing the player's name – and numbered stocking tabs. Whilst some pundits criticised the initiatives, Arthur Haddock, writing in the *Yorkshire Evening Post*, congratulated the club for 'displaying a flair of salesmanship that will have great repercussions in the sporting world'.

Today, nobody would make a fuss, but in 1972 we were the first team to perform pre-match routines. Our supporters loved the gimmicks, especially the stocking tabs, but as usual, we got a bit of stick from certain sections of the press.

With a place in the semi-final assured, it was back to League action in the race for the title alongside Derby County, Manchester City and Liverpool. Following a crucial defeat at Derby, Leeds bounced back with victories over Huddersfield and Stoke, but at a heavy price, because Terry Cooper broke a leg at the Victoria Ground just a week before their semi-final clash with Birmingham City. Undeterred, Leeds arrived at Hillsborough determined to make no mistakes.

Our pre-match meeting took its usual format. Don never made anything complicated; he went round players individually, giving us our own specific instructions. He went through a dossier on our opponents, how they played and how we should mark them. Some cynics ridiculed them, but the boss left nothing to chance,

Derby delight – Mick scores against West Yorkshire neighbours Huddersfield Town.

he wanted us to know as much as possible about our opponents. He did make one crucial change though, when he decided to play David Harvey in goal. Gary had missed the previous game through injury and David had been superb. Over the years Gary had made mistakes, clearly Don wasn't prepared to take a chance any more. It was a massive opportunity for David, and he took his chance.

The match went well from the beginning. We were determined to get a grip early on and soon broke through when I scored. A few minutes later Peter Lorimer added a second, which knocked the stuffing out of them. I grabbed a second midway through the second half to seal a comfortable win.

Leeds' victory had been clinically achieved. Mike Casey in the *Yorkshire Evening Post* analysed each player's performance after the win. He had this to say about Leeds two-goal hero Mick Jones, 'it was wonderful to see the energetic, fearless striker notch two goals after all his hard work this season. So often criticised for his lack of scoring power, he answered the best answer to the "knockers". His play off the ball caused tension in the City defence, a big factor in United's victory.'

'Sniffer' Clarke sets up his partner for the first goal against Birmingham City.

Knockout punch – Leeds are on their way to Wembley.

After their emphatic win, it was back to League action. Unfortunately, Leeds lost at Newcastle, but followed that up with victories over West Brom and Chelsea. Leeds still had one League match to go, at Wolves, which the FA ruled would have to take place forty-eight hours after the cup final against Arsenal.

The build up to the cup final was hectic. We were fitted for our suits and recorded our cup final song. Les Reed came over to the ground where we rehearsed 'Leeds, Leeds, Leeds' a couple of times, before travelling over to a studio in Manchester. None of the lads fancied standing in front of the microphone, so I was pushed forward as lead singer, they said they'd back me up! It was great fun, and the song is still popular at Elland Road today, but is better known as 'Marching on Together'.

Like all the lads, I couldn't wait for the final. The cup final defeat against Chelsea still rankled with us; we were determined not to slip up again. It would be close, because Arsenal were a good side, but we fancied our chances. Of course we realised the double was only two matches away, but we could not think that far ahead.

The night before the game we played bingo and carpet bowls before watching a video of the Southampton win. As usual, one of Don's friends, Herbert Warner, was helping to relax us. As a player I got more stick than most, but Herbert got even more than I did, and took it brilliantly. He would tell us jokes; play cards, call out the bingo numbers and was great to have around. We were positive and relaxed.

Pop stars!

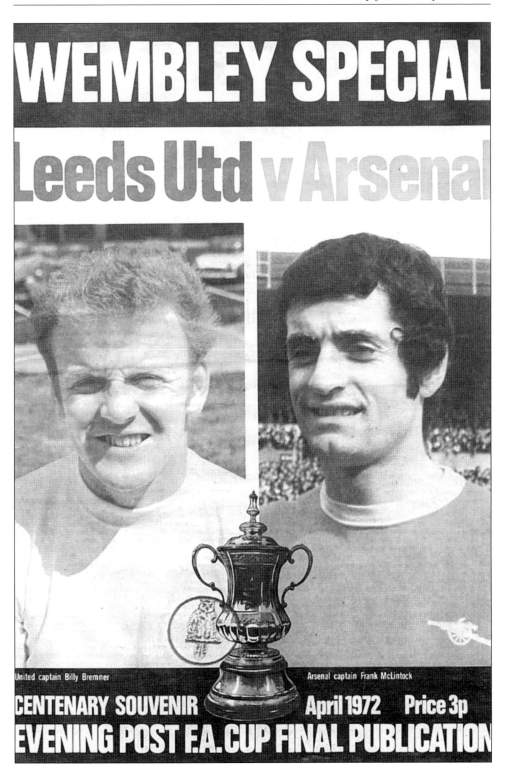

Yorkshire Evening Post FA Cup final special.

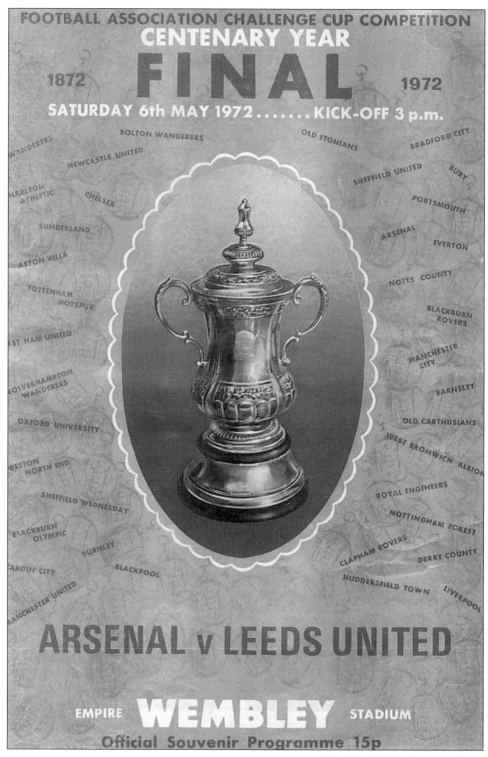

Match programme for the 1972 FA Cup final.

EMPIRE STADIUM · WEMBLEY

The Football Association
Challenge Cup Competition

FINAL TIE

SATURDAY, MAY 6, 1972
KICK-OFF 3 p.m.

J.S. Lill CHAIRMAN:
WEMBLEY STADIUM LTD

PASS TO DRESSING ROOM

Available at Dressing Room Entrance
between B and C Turnstiles only.

NOT TRANSFERABLE

TO BE RETAINED   (See Plan on back)

Destiny awaits.

On the day, naturally, there was that extra buzz of excitement, but Don tried to keep
to our normal routine. After our pre-match meal, we watched 'cup final' Grandstand
before his main team-talk. We went through the dossier of Arsenal's players and our
game tactics, then set off for Wembley. I played three-card brag on the coach with Billy,
Allan and Peter; as usual I lost!

Arsenal v Leeds United, 1972 FA Cup final:

Arsenal: Barnett, Rice, McNab, Storey, McLintock (captain), Simpson, Armstrong, Ball, Radford, Graham, George; sub: Kennedy.
Leeds United: Harvey, Reaney, Madeley, Bremner (captain), Charlton, Hunter, Lorimer, Clarke, Jones, Giles, Gray; sub: Bates.

The journey was great, especially when we turned into Wembley Way; the sight of all the fans was fantastic. We had a walk around the pitch; all the Arsenal lads were dressed casually, which surprised us a bit. The conditions were very different to 1970. It was hot and the pitch was absolutely immaculate. It's not like any other pitch we played on during the season; it was so spongy. Before long we were back in the dressing room. Don said a few last words of encouragement before it was time to go.

Waiting in the tunnel was really nerve-wracking: you wait for a while, which is the worst part because all you want to do is get out onto the pitch and get on with it. Standing there, all you see is a little light in the distance. As you walk towards it, it gets bigger and wider. Coming out of the tunnel the roar is unbelievable; the adrenaline rush is just incredible.

Although I'd played in a cup final before, it seemed different because we were playing

Bertie Mee and Don Revie lead their teams out for the Centenary Cup Final.

on a 'proper' Wembley pitch. It was also the competition's centenary year, so there was a pageant as we walked out. After meeting the dignitaries, we ran off for the kick-in. All my nerves disappeared.

The first half went reasonably well, with both sides having chances. Alan Ball hit a screamer that Paul Reaney cleared off the line and David Harvey saved smartly from a Frank McLintock free kick. I just missed with an effort that shaved the post and Clarkie had a couple of chances. Don didn't say much at half time. He just told us to keep at it, we were the better side and he felt sure a goal would come. It was going to be tight, so we knew we had to take one of the few chances that came our way.

Eight minutes into the half Leeds broke through:

Peter Lorimer slipped a ball to me on the right hand side. As I approached Arsenal's full-back, Bob McNab, I decided to take him on and get to the by-line. Going past him I had a little bit of luck because the ball ricocheted off his legs and bobbled the right way for me. McNab knew it was a dangerous attacking position – he muttered in no uncertain terms how lucky I was! When I was in this situation, I always aimed for the penalty spot. The ball was away from the goalkeeper's reach, and with defender's running back towards their goal anything could happen.

I whipped in a good cross; Clarkie came flying in. He was going to volley the ball, but the ball dipped at the last moment, so he dived instead. He got a perfect connection and it fitted perfectly in the far corner… we were one up! Allan came running over to celebrate and all the lads joined in. It was a fantastic feeling.

Jogging back to the centre-circle I realised there was a long way to go, both teams would undoubtedly get chances to score, but deep down I knew we had a great chance because I couldn't see our defence letting them back into the game. Arsenal did have the odd half chance, but we were by far the better team in the second half and should really have scored a second before the end.

Before long we had a signal from the bench that there was little time remaining when suddenly a ball was played through to me in a dangerous position. I went past Peter Simpson and saw Arsenal's keeper Geoff Barnett come out to narrow the angle; I had a half-chance to score. I tried to nick the ball past him, but tumbled over the top of him and automatically put my left arm down to break my fall.

The pain was unbearable. Unbeknown to me I'd dislocated my elbow. On any other pitch this injury would not have occurred. Throughout my career I had similar falls without any problems, but the soft Wembley pitch caused the damage. I could hear Barnett saying get up you soft so and so, but he soon realised I wasn't joking because I was screaming in pain.

Les Cocker and Doc Adams came over. Les had a quick look and told me I'd have to be carried off, Doc Adams confirmed I had to go straight to the dressing room. I told them no way. I realised we'd won the cup, and I wanted to receive my medal from the Queen. As a player, one of my greatest ambitions was to receive a cup winner's medal, and no injury was going to stop me. I told them to get me on my feet; I'd manage to walk across. Eventually they agreed but Doc Adams insisted on coming with me.

After they strapped my arm around my body, I slowly got up and began to walk across the pitch. I thought I'd collapse. I had no idea at the time that Billy had already collected the FA Cup and the lads had been up for their medals. All I knew was that I was determined to climb up to the Royal Box to receive my medal from the Queen. I only found out later that I'd kept her waiting for ten minutes.

As we got to the bottom of the steps Mick Bates came over and told me he had my medal, but I still wanted to meet the Queen. I could just see Glenis and all the families on the right hand side. Norman came over and helped me up the steps. Everyone was slinging their arms around me; Glenis was in tears. At the top of the stairs, I nearly collapsed again. We walked across the Royal Box and everyone shook my hand. When I approached the Queen, I heard her say that she had nothing to give me. She shook my hand and asked me how I was. I felt awful, but fortunately, I was still in enough control to give her a polite reply!

We walked to the end of the Royal Box and had to stand for the National Anthem. Once again, I thought I was going to collapse. Somehow, I got to the bottom of the stairs where Doc Adams and the ambulance men were waiting with a stretcher. When we approached the tunnel end where the Leeds fans were situated, the reception was unbelievable. The supporters were chanting my name, 'MI...MIC...MICK...Mick Jones!' These are moments I'll never forget.

We got to the dressing room and I rested on the treatment table. They needed four doctors to put my arm back into place. Two stood at the bottom and two at the top, I could feel my elbow snap back in. All the lads came over to see how I was, but they knew there was nothing they could do. Before long, they all went off to Wolverhampton for the League game on the Monday night, whereas I went back to our hotel in London with Doc Adams and Glenis. We watched the game on Match of the Day, but I barely slept that night. Next morning Doc Adams drove us back to Leeds.

There was no question that the best team on the day won.

Alan Hoby, *Sunday Express*: 'The elegant stylists of Leeds have won the FA Cup for the first time. Whatever happens the beaten finalists of 1965 and 1970 have at last killed the sneer that they always stumble at the final hurdle. That taunt lies buried forever beneath the damp green turf of Wembley.'

GREEN POST

SATURDAY MAY 6 1972   No. 26,984   Tel: LEEDS 32701   Price 3p.

Leeds United supporters with plenty to shout about in Trafalgar Square.

IT'S YOURS, UNITED

£5,000 and car in Pick the Spot

Pages 2 and 9

Free transfer for cup hero and Storrie

Geoff Barnett, Arsenal goalkeeper, saves from Mick Jones, Leeds United centre-forward, in the Cup Final at Wembley. The United players on the left are Peter Lorimer and Allan Clarke.

FRANCIS ACCEPTS

SCOTTISH CUP FINAL

RESULT:—
CELTIC 1
HIBERNIAN 0

Clarke header brings Cup to Elland Road: 1-0

CUP WINNERS AT LAST! LEEDS UNITED WON THE F.A. CUP CENTENARY FINAL AGAINST ARSENAL AT WEMBLEY BY 1-0.

By DON WARTERS

Reaney 'rescue act' yet again

By MIKE CASEY

Conteh sprints to hat-trick

Few chances

Desperate lunge

Death ends family Cup Final plan

SAW CRASHED CAR

David Harvey, Leeds goalkeeper, safely gathers the ball in the Cup Final, to close attentions are Charlie George, Arsenal centre-forward, and Norman Hunter, Leeds United left-half.

Cricket scores

LEAGUE CUP

RESULT:—
LEEDS UNITED ... 1
ARSENAL 0

Aussie Soccer Results

At last…

What a goal!

A moment Leeds United fans will treasure is captured by the camera.

Allan Clarke's superb goal which brought the F.A. Cup to Elland Road for the first time in the club's history.

With Arsenal skipper Frank McLintock (left) and his colleague Peter Simpson (No. 6) helpless bystanders as the ball flashes past the outstretched arms of 'keeper Geoff Barnett, United's captain Billy Bremner is on the spot to savour the shot which sent United's supporters roaring their appreciation.

Clarke's match-winning effort — which crowned an England-class performance by United's striker — came in the 53rd minute.

Jack Charlton began the move with a pass to winger Peter Lorimer, who flicked the ball to centre-forward Mick Jones on the right flank.

Jones tore past Huddersfield-born Bob McNab before centering for Clarke to beat the Arsenal 'keeper with a brilliant header.

The brilliantly-executed goal deserved to win the 100th F.A. Cup Final and earn its scorer the "Man of the match" award for the second time in his career.

The previous occasion Clarke was a member of the Leicester City side beaten by Manchester City in 1969. This time the story had a happy ending for the lethal six-footer.

A split second from victory. Allan Clarke's whip-crack header delivered from a full 16 yards zooms towards the Arsenal net. Geoff Barnett is airborne, arms outstretched, but, as Clarke said later, he did not have a chance. Peter Simpson is the defender on the left and Billy Bremner (inevitably) is near the action.

The despair of Arsenal goalkeeper Geoff Barnett as Peter Simpson bends to pick the ball out of the net.

Scorer Allan Clarke and Mick Jones, who made the vital goal, share the precious moment.

A picture taken from a different angle. Peter Lorimer was first to congratulate the jubilant Allan Clarke. But there is anguish on the face of Frank McLintock (left) and George Graham (right). In the background, Leeds fans stand to salute their heroes.

Jones … Clarke … 1-0.

Hugh McIlvanney, *Observer*: 'Don Revie's Leeds United, the team who had come to regard Wembley as a place of near misses, won the FA Cup at their third attempt yesterday, when they outplayed Arsenal to an extent that was inadequately reflected in the scoreline. It was Leeds whose football was more controlled, whose ideas the more inventive. Once Leeds had settled, and especially after their goal, they dominated Arsenal confidently.'

Frank Butler, *News of the World*: 'Leeds well deserved their victory after they got out of the Yale-lock grip of the Arsenal defensive system in the first half. A goal was needed to break the Arsenal system and what a great goal Leeds scored. Leeds had always looked the more classy footballing side. Once they scored they blossomed out like superman. Suddenly Arsenal looked tired, beaten and very ordinary.

David Miller, *Sunday Telegraph*: 'Leeds, the most consistent team in European soccer for the last eight years, carried off the centenary FA Cup in a final which was eventually one-sided. From the start Leeds were transparently the better side and by the finish they had outplayed the opposition in almost every phase of the game, even if they only controlled it for that last half-hour.'

Frank McGhee, *Sunday Mirror*: 'Arsenal could have tried for another 100 years and still would not have a serious chance of beating Leeds. Not on the form, the mood and the manpower seen in this centenary cup final.'

Albert Barham, *Guardian*: 'A new name, Leeds United will be inscribed on the plinth of the FA Cup this centenary year and few will deny that the honour has been long overdue. A spectacularly headed goal by Clarke was insufficient reward for the superiority of Leeds in every department of the game. They could and should have had a couple more afterwards.'

Terry Brindle, *Yorkshire Post*: 'It was the day on which Leeds United proved beyond question that they are a great side. A day on which the most coveted trophy in soccer was added to their impressive pedigree, and no side which has not won the cup can claim to true greatness.'

Looking back, I'm sorry I missed the final whistle, the celebrations, going up for the cup and the lap of honour, but I was pleased I'd achieved one of my greatest ambitions. However, most disappointing I was out of the clash with Wolves. Even though I couldn't play, I was not going to miss the game. Doc Adams collected me from my house. On the journey down the M1, I have never seen so many Leeds fans in cars with scarves draped from the windows. It was chock-a-block all the way to Wolverhampton, and an incredible sight.

When we got to the ground thousands were locked out. I eventually got in and went to see the lads in the dressing room. It was obvious Eddie, John and Allan should not have been playing, but they had to. Playing at Wembley really takes it out of you; the players who were carrying knocks were simply unable to recover in forty-eight hours. I couldn't get a seat for the game, so stood in a little press box behind the goal.

On a night of unbelievable tension, Leeds fought to the end, and but for diabolical refereeing would have won this match, the Championship and the double. Writing in the *Yorkshire Evening Post*, Don Warters commented, 'if ever a team had cause to feel bitter, United have today'. In a never-say-die performance, Leeds should have been awarded three penalties. Warters added that this must have felt like 'knives being driven slowly into their backs'. Although Leeds lost the match 2-1, the city of Leeds was proud of the team's achievements and organised a fantastic civic reception.

The defeat at Wolves was heartbreaking, we'd worked so hard to get back into the title race, it was so disappointing. I've never known a quieter dressing room. It was far worse than 1970 because we really deserved the double that season. We were by far the most adventurous and entertaining team.

It was so upsetting to see nine months' work destroyed by poor fixture planning by the FA. The closure of the ground at the beginning of the season had proved costly, but the

Recuperating after the Cup Final.

Leeds United, 1972 FA Cup winners. From left to right, back row: Reaney, Charlton, Harvey, Jones, Hunter, Madeley. Front row: Lorimer, Clarke, Bremner, Giles, Bates, Gray.

FA's decision to play the final game so close to the FA Cup final ultimately cost the title. It was hard enough playing against teams when we had time to prepare, because they always raised their game, which was fine; we were their match of the season, but to have only forty-eight hours to recover from the final was so unjust.

Watching was probably worse than playing, because you could see we weren't going to do it, even though the lads gave everything. If the game had been played a couple of days later, we'd have clinched the double, I'm convinced of that.

The reception our supporters gave us at Elland Road, and through the streets when we paraded the FA Cup, was unbelievable and something I'll never forget. Looking back, I'm so pleased we managed to win the FA Cup, because it was such a big ambition for us all, and to achieve it in the competitions centenary year was superb.

10

MONTY'S SAVE AND GREEK TRAGEDY
1972/73

Whilst the majority of the first-team squad enjoyed a well-deserved break, Mick Jones began his rehabilitation program in a bid to get fit for the new season.

Throughout the summer, I went in each day for physiotherapy. Things went well, and I was confident I'd be ready for pre-season training. The club as usual held trials for new apprentices. I'd never watched the whole process before; I found it fascinating. The trials had certainly moved on since my day, they lasted two weeks with three thousand hopefuls trying to make it in the game. The success Don Revie had brought to the club meant that Leeds United could attract the best young talent around, although there was no guarantee the youngsters would make it.

Don supervised the various stages. The trials lasted two weeks, after a week eight hundred remained. Two hundred stayed for the last few days, then on the final day the best ones played in trial matches. From all the hopefuls five joined the ground staff as apprentices, but none of them were offered professional terms at seventeen, which just illustrates how difficult it is to become a professional footballer.

Mick made it back into the starting line-up when the new campaign began, but an injury in the opening game at Chelsea forced him to miss the first month of the season. Although results were encouraging, performances had not hit the heights of the previous season. In his absence the balance of the side was not right, a point acknowledged by skipper Billy Bremner in an interview with a national paper.

'His sort of game is invaluable to the rest of us. He's always running to create space and is never far away when a team-mate's in trouble and needs a "get-out". That sort of dedication and commitment to a team demands a lot of qualities. You need the heart the size of a football, the guts of a Zatopek, and more than anything you must be the fittest man on the books… the sooner he's back the more confident every Leeds player will feel.'

Leeds United, 1972/73. From left to right, back row: Cherry, Madeley, Jones, Ellam, Jordan, Charlton. Middle row: Reaney, Galvin, Harvey, Sprake, Hunter, Clarke. Front row: Lorimer, Giles, Bremner, Bates, Gray, Yorath.

On his return Mick scored in four of his first five games back, including a spectacular overhead kick in a 2-1 defeat by Liverpool. Incredibly though, following the loss some pundits were writing the team off. Eric Todd of the *Guardian* wrote, 'I think they must accept that Giles and Charlton are past their peak, and that Bremner's overworked batteries are running low… Leeds have achieved many things but now… the writing is on the wall'.

I didn't read the papers all the time, but we were aware what people were saying. It was ludicrous; we knew we had a lot to offer still. We bounced back immediately by defeating the defending champions Derby County 5-0 and one of the front runners Everton 2-1.

The media was fickle. Following the win at Goodison, Norman Wynne wrote, 'Laugh off any suggestion that Leeds are slipping. They dismissed Everton as a team of championship hopefuls with a display of efficient football that was almost as colourful as their all-yellow strip'. The results were the springboard to a sixteen-match run, which would bring just a single defeat. Six victories at the turn of the year put Leeds back among the pacemakers again. However, there were echoes of 1970 as Leeds made progress in the FA Cup and European Cup Winners Cup.

In Europe, Leeds had overcome the intimidating atmosphere of Ankara, squeezing home 2-1 on aggregate before facing a tough trip behind the Iron Curtain in the next

What a goal… Mick strikes with a spectacular overhead kick against Liverpool.

Happy New Year – Mick's fine header defeats Tottenham.

It's tight, but Mick scores the winner against West Ham.

Mick keeps his eyes on the ball as he shakes off a Chelsea defender.

round against East German side Carl Zeiss Jena. After another creditable draw on their travels, the team was thankful for their home form for a 2-0 aggregate win. The quarter-final against Rapid Bucharest however was far more comfortable; a 5-0 win in the opening leg making the return a formality. Before the semi-final there was the little matter of the FA Cup.

The campaign had been a tortuous affair to begin with, Norwich City proving very difficult opponents to get by. It took three games to make it through to the next round before we had relatively comfortable wins over Plymouth Argyle and West Brom, which set up a quarter-final encounter with Brian Clough's Derby County team. We were determined to win after they pipped us to the title the previous season.

Leeds were indebted to a Peter Lorimer special for their place in the semi-finals, and Lorimer was quick to praise the maker of the goal – Mick Jones. 'It was a great ball… he picked me out and laid it in front of me. I knew it was in as soon as I struck it.'

Many pundits believed this would be their hardest game of the season. Barry Foster of the *Yorkshire Post* thought Leeds had been in 'invincible mood, complete in every department… once Peter Lorimer had supplied the killer punch, Derby might as well have put their clocks on there and then for British Summer Time and gone home'.
In the semi-finals, we faced Wolves at Maine Road, which gave us a chance to avenge

This header gave Leeds an aggregate win over Ankaragucu in the Cup-Winners Cup.

Mick pounces on a rebound from 'Hotshot' Lorimer to knock out Carl Zeiss Jena.

Leeds cruise past Rapid Bucharest in the quarter-finals.

our League defeat that cost us the double. As with the Derby game we were really fired up, even though we had a few regulars out. Unfortunately it got worse when Big Jack had to go off during the first half, this meant we had to reshuffle our defence with Norman out injured. Paul Madeley and Terry Yorath paired up, but we were used to adapting. Wolves probably thought we'd be weakened, but the pair of them were superb. Gradually we got on top and Billy scored the all-important goal, the third time he'd struck the winner in an FA Cup semi-final for us, which was some achievement.

Following the win against Wolves, the treble was within reach. Once again, the team was winning national approval. Derek Wallis, *Daily Mirror*, 'Leeds United can now claim to be arguably the greatest team English football has known. Greater even than the phenomenal Arsenal team of the '30s, than Spurs of the early 1960s, greater even than Manchester United of so many post war years. Love them or hate them, and curiously there are still more ready to swear at them than by them, there can be no dispute that Leeds are the team of at least the last decade... The greatest English club team ever? I wouldn't argue against it.'

Four days after their win over Wolves, Leeds attempted to reach their second cup final of the season against the crack Yugoslavian side Hadjuk Split.

Bremner strikes against Wolves in the FA Cup semi-final.

Next stop Wembley!

The first leg was a tense affair, which we just shaded – thanks to a goal from Allan. However, it had come at a price because he was later sent off when he retaliated to a vicious challenge by a Split defender, and would miss the second leg and final if we got there. In the return, we drew 0-0 to reach another European final – unfortunately, a booking for Billy meant that he would also miss the final against AC Milan.

The effort in reaching the two finals finally caught up with the players, Leeds ended the season in third place, due to one win in their next six League games. The week before the cup final, with their League challenge over, Revie played only Peter Lorimer from his first team squad against Birmingham City as his team rested.

Before the cup final with Sunderland we were odds-on favourites to win, no one gave them a chance. However, we knew it would be tough – after all, they had knocked out Manchester City and Arsenal on the way to the final. Nevertheless, we were confident. We followed the same routine as the previous season and all felt relaxed. This was my third final in four seasons; I knew the pressures and felt extremely comfortable leading up to the game.

This is becoming a pleasant habit – Mick's third FA Cup final in four years.

Sunderland v Leeds United, 1973 FA Cup final:

Sunderland: Montgomery, Malone, Guthrie, Horswill, Watson, Pitt, Kerr (captain), Hughes, Halom, Porterfield, Tueart; sub: Young.
Leeds United: Harvey, Reaney, Cherry, Bremner (captain), Madeley, Hunter, Lorimer, Clarke, Jones, Giles, Gray; sub: Yorath.

The 1973 FA Cup final has gone down in history as the biggest upset ever. Everyone connected with Leeds was naturally shattered, but handled the 1-0 defeat graciously. Don Revie commented: 'Give credit to Sunderland, they were full of enthusiasm and running. We are making no excuses.' Disappointed and defiant, Revie added, 'We'll be back again; we start in July.'

For Derek Wallis of the *Daily Mirror* the FA Cup would never be the same again. 'The harsh, fiercely competitive world of football, which breeds giants sparingly and their conquerors occasionally, is still in a state of shock following the most sensational FA Cup result of all time. If a Second Division team of limited experience can beat First Division opposition of such stature at Wembley there are no giants left to be killed anywhere else.'

For some reason we all had an off day, but I still felt we should have won, we had enough chances. Sunderland played well, but after they scored, we failed to pick ourselves up. Even so, Peter Lorimer should have scored. How Jim Montgomery saved his point-blank shot I'll never know. It's still one of the most famous saves in the British game – only Gordon Banks' save from Pele in the 1970 World Cup

The greatest ever save? Montomery wins the FA Cup for Sunderland.

finals surpasses it. If Peter's shot had gone in I'm convinced we'd have won, but it wasn't to be.

People often say that 'a team's name is stamped on the cup', but that was no consolation at the time. In the dressing room afterwards we were absolutely distraught and could not believe how much we'd under-performed. The look on our supporters' faces after the game when we left the ground is something I've never forgotten. We let our supporters and ourselves down.

Following the defeat Leeds travelled to Salonika to face AC Milan in the European Cup Winners Cup final. The players were unsettled by newspaper stories the day before the game saying that Don Revie was to quit and join Everton. It was even reported in the *Yorkshire Post* that Revie had told his players he was '95 per cent certain' he would go, which could have done little for morale before such an important match.

AC Milan v Leeds United, 1973 European Cup Winners Cup final:

AC Milan: Veechi, Sabadini, Zignoli, Anquilletti, Turone, Rosato (sub. Dolci), Sogliano, Benetti, Bigon, Rivera, Chiarugi.
Leeds United: Harvey, Reaney, Cherry, Bates, Yorath, Hunter, Lorimer, Jordan, Jones, Gray F (sub. McQueen), Madeley.

The final was ruined by a scandalous performance by the referee. Some of the decisions Christos Michas made were unbelievable; his bias towards the Italians was outrageous, especially when he turned down three blatant penalties for Leeds. Michas never officiated in a professional match again.

It was a tragic end to a season that had promised so much. Don Revie had 'never been more proud' of his team, who although lacking a number of key players had outplayed AC Milan 'in every department'. As for the refereeing, Revie lamented. 'How many times has this happened to us? There was the West Brom affair... the Wolves match last season. We played so well tonight and got nothing for it.'

The players won enormous praise for their efforts.

Derek Wallis in the *Mirror* wrote, 'For a team to go out for such a crucial match stripped of four great players and challenge a team of Milan's status so nearly successfully was nothing short of miraculous.' Unfortunately, there was only 'heartbreak for Leeds and another heartbreak for Revie... from players who gave him everything they had and more.'

Wallis concluded, 'the catcalls, barracking and general disapproval continued as Milan took the trophy on a lap of honour. Rather it should be a lap of dishonour. The crowd was prepared to forgive Hunter's action when he retaliated... they were not prepared to forgive and forget Milan's cynicism in the form of provocative challenges as the game approached its end.'

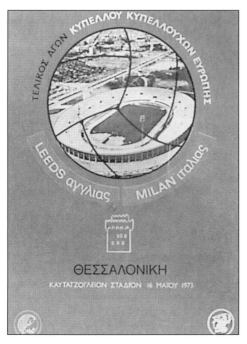

Left: Double disaster. Right: Time to reflect on an eventful season. Mick relaxes with Lindsey and Mark.

Against AC Milan, I played against one of the hardest players I've ever faced. A thunderstorm broke out when we kicked off, and from the first minute their centre-back elbowed me, punched me in the back, spat in my face; he even tried to gouge my eyes; it was unbelievable. He was giving me a real hard time, but the referee did nothing. They scored early on from a dubious free kick, and we were struggling to get back into the game.

As we were walking off at half time, I was not happy. Playing in Europe was different, I loved the challenge, but I was getting nowhere. Norman asked me what the problem was. I told him this fellow was giving me a nightmare game, but I couldn't do anything with him. Norman told me to bring him down his end. Early in the second half this Italian went for a fifty-fifty with Norman, not a good idea! Norman thundered in with a powerful challenge and looked at me, put his thumbs up in the air – 'Alright pal!'

I had a better second half but for most of the game they had eight defending at all times, which in the end proved too much. That said, the decisions that went against us were scandalous. We never stood a chance, the refereeing was appalling, and the worst I'd ever experienced. The reception we received from the Greek supporters was incredible; but it didn't take away the disappointment we felt afterwards in the dressing room. To lose two cup finals in a few days was heart-breaking, but I was confident we could pick ourselves up again.

11
CHAMPIONS AGAIN
1973/74

Following the double cup-final disappointment, the general consensus within the media was that Leeds United were a spent force. One report highlighted the cup final defeat by Sunderland as the final blow to Don Revie's great side. 'Sunderland smashed the most consistent team of the last decade such a shattering blow to pride, composure and self-respect that the cracks will not be easily repaired. It may well be that Leeds can never completely recover this time; can never climb back to where they were, what they were.'

Leeds United 1973/74. From left to right, back row: Lorimer, Gray E., Bates, Clarke, Hunter, McQueen, Ellam, Reaney, Gray F. Front row: Yorath, Sprake, Cherry, Jordan, Giles, Harvey, Madeley, Bremner, Jones.

Before the start of the 1973/74 campaign everyone wrote us off, it was incredible. However we weren't finished, the likes of Joe Jordan and Gordon McQueen were breaking into the side and a number of the more experienced players had a lot of life in them yet. We'd tasted disappointment before, and whenever we had our backs to the wall that was when we were at our most dangerous.

Just before the first game of the season at home to Everton, we had a team meeting as usual in the players' lounge. Don went through our match tactics, then stunned us all. He said, 'Right lads, I believe we're capable of going through an entire season unbeaten'. We all looked at one another. He said, 'I'm serious, we're going again for the League title but I also believe we can remain unbeaten. Everyone's written us off, you've all seen the reports, I believe in you and we're going to show everyone that we're still the best.' Billy looked at him and said, 'The whole season... you're joking boss'. Don made it clear that he wasn't, he told us we had the ability to do this, and he wanted us to slam the reporters' words down their throats that we were finished, and prove them all wrong.

Leeds won their opening seven games against Everton 3-1 Arsenal 2-1, Tottenham 3-0, Wolves 4-1, Birmingham 3-0, Wolves 2-0 and Southampton 2-1. Mick grabbed his third goal of the season at Wolves, a match that created a club record sixth consecutive win from the start of the season; the pundits down south were well and truly put in their place.

After each game, opposing managers were full of praise. The win at Tottenham may have been only the third match of the season, but manager Bill Nicholson conceded that 'Leeds are a great side... the best in the country'. Freddie Goodwin, Birmingham's manager, was similarly impressed: 'Leeds are a great side who are going to take an awful lot of stopping. They are better than England in some ways. Here you've got an all-international outfit with the wonderful blend that comes from playing together for so long.'

The winning run ended when an ultra-defensive Manchester United eked out a draw at Elland Road. As the unbeaten run continued, Mick was enjoying his best start to a League campaign since joining Leeds in 1967, scoring eight goals in the opening fourteen matches, including five in as many games against Stoke, Leicester City, Liverpool and West Ham (a game in which he scored a brace). Only a third of the season had gone, but Leeds were already six points clear of their nearest challengers.

In the thrilling clash against Liverpool, a classic header from Mick won a pulsating match. Milan Milanic, coach to Red Star Belgrade, who was at the game, thought his goal 'was skilfully worked and brilliantly scored... a goal reminiscent of Garrincha and Pele at work for Brazil'. Praise indeed.

Following Mick's double against the Hammers in a 4-1 win, their manager Ron Greenwood was convinced the title race was all but over. 'Leeds are the equal of Manchester United in their heyday. They play with such skill imagination and flair. It looks as if they are out on their own, playing the sort of football I would love to play.'

Off to a flyer – Mick scores against Everton on the opening day of the season.

This goal against Wolves makes it four consecutive wins.

Mick in action against Birmingham.

Party poopers – Manchester United end the winning sequence.

A goal against Stoke.

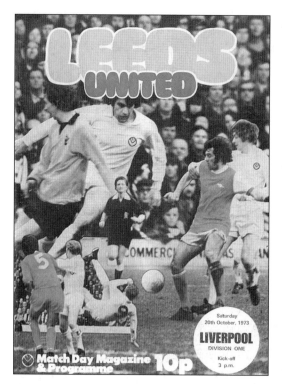

Mick's header wins a crucial match.

After the flak we'd received, our start took everyone by surprise. Everywhere we went as usual there were packed houses, and we played some wonderful football; nobody could live with us. It didn't matter who we were playing, we felt confident and thought we'd win.

Pundits and managers were calling for Mick's return to the England squad. Revie naturally gave him his vote 'because of his overall work rate, heading ability and ball control. He also knows Allan Clarke's style of play so well'. Wolves' manager Bill McGarry was also convinced on the Clarke-Jones partnership. 'On current form I don't think there's a better front two in the business. Jones makes Clarke play; he's everything you want from a centre forward. He's brave, never stops running and takes up some tremendous positions.' Freddie Goodwin added: 'Jones has always been a very under-rated player. A lot of his work doesn't get the appreciation it deserves, but he's a manager's player and a player's player.'

Following a 2-2 draw with QPR, consecutive wins in December over Ipswich Town, Chelsea, Norwich City and Newcastle United meant Leeds were now nine points clear of the chasing pack. The 2-1 win at Stamford Bridge set a post-war record of twenty games unbeaten from the start of a Football League campaign. By New Year, all bets were off on Leeds winning the title. Indeed, you could get 25-1 against the team remaining undefeated for the rest of the season. Playing with style, the team was receiving national acclaim.

Frank McGhee of the *Mirror* could not think of a better club side in post-war football. 'Leeds are in grave danger of being more admired, acclaimed and loved more universally than this much-maligned team would have dared to dream a few years back.'

Hammered! Mick puts Leeds 2-0 up against West Ham.

Mick wheels away after scoring.

Another two points in the bag.

Thanks Peter!

Joe Jordan acclaims Mick's ninth goal of the season, against QPR.

Merry Christmas everybody – it certainly was at Elland Road.

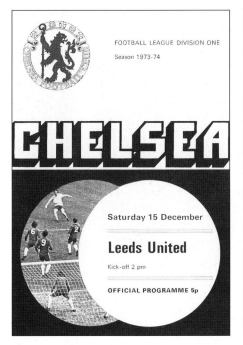

Left: Record breakers. Right: 29 games undefeated, a match which saw Mick score his last goal for Leeds.

With every team in the League desperate to beat Leeds, each match became more intense. After the draw at St James Park on Boxing Day, four of the next five matches ended in draws, the only victory coming against Southampton, before consecutive wins over Arsenal and Manchester United took the run to 29 games undefeated. A 2-0 win at Old Trafford (a match in which Mick, as it transpired, scored his last goal as a professional footballer) took Leeds to within a match of equalling the record unbeaten run from the beginning of a Division One campaign, set by Burnley in 1920/21.

Having gone out of the League Cup and UEFA Cup at an early stage, we were one of the favourites to lift the FA Cup, but surprisingly lost to Bristol City at Elland Road in a fifth round. We were now free to 'concentrate on the League', but we were picking up a lot of injuries. I soon joined the list.

Following the defeat by Bristol, we prepared for our clash with Stoke City. During a five-a-side match I suddenly had an unbelievable pain in my left knee. I couldn't move; the trainers had to escort me off the pitch. The doctor looked at my knee in the dressing room but wasn't sure what damage might have occurred. The pain reduced enough for me to get changed.

All eyes are on Southampton 'keeper Eric Martin as he tips Lorimer's thunderbolt over the bar.

Mick puts Leeds a goal up against the Saints – sadly this was his last at Elland Road.

Bristol City clear in the closing minutes to knock Leeds out of the FA Cup.

On my way home, I had to call into Headingley briefly. I parked the car and started to walk across the main crossroads when a sudden pain again in my knee immobilised me. With traffic coming both ways a couple of people came over and helped me back to my car. I knew there was something seriously wrong. Somehow, I got home and went down to the ground next morning, but doctors were still unsure what was wrong. I couldn't train and missed the next month's games.

Leeds unbeaten record went at Stoke City when they lost 3-2. It was the start of a worrying spell that would bring just one win in seven games, including four defeats!

At Stoke, we should never have lost after taking a two-goal lead. Nevertheless, it had been an unbelievable run and we'd set a new club record. Unfortunately, we began to go through a lean spell, confidence had taken a knock and injuries were really beginning to take their toll. We were still top, but Liverpool were closing the gap. I was nowhere near fit, but Don wanted me to play. I couldn't train properly; all I was able to do was some jogging. I came on as substitute for three games, which we lost, but it was impossible; I had to rest.

Following the last of Mick's appearances, at West Ham, there was a real danger that the title was going to slip away as Liverpool could mathematically overhaul Leeds.

Despite the setbacks, we were still confident we'd win the title. Liverpool had to win their remaining matches to pip us, which was a hard task. Although I couldn't play, we got back to winning ways with a crucial win against Derby County. Liverpool then dropped vital points in two of their matches in hand; we had the initiative back.

We were due to play Sheffield United at Elland Road with only four games remaining, and knew a couple of wins would probably tie up the title. With Joe Jordan, who had deputised for me, out injured Don was desperate for me to play. Even though I'd done no training, I agreed. We drew 0-0, but would have won but for a terrible decision by the referee when he disallowed an effort by Peter Lorimer. Allan Clarke had strayed into an offside position but there was no way he was interfering with play. We were livid after the match. The only consolation was that even though Liverpool could tie on points with us, our goal average was superior, however we knew there was no room for any more slips.

Twenty-four hours later Leeds faced Sheffield United again.

The afternoon of the game I was sat with Allan at our hotel in Sheffield relaxing with my leg on a chair when suddenly a lump came up at the back of my knee. I showed

Leeds go close against Sheffield United during the title run-in.

Allan, and he said you better get Les Cocker and Don Revie to have a look. They told me to try not worrying about it, which wasn't easy.

Don made me captain because it was my first League game at Bramall Lane since joining Leeds. I went out and gave everything, but a few minutes from time I waved to come off. I got a standing ovation from both sets of supporters, which meant a lot, but I was shattered. We won the match 2-0; Peter Lorimer grabbed both goals in the second half. Afterwards everyone congratulated me. The result was crucial because Liverpool had also won on the same evening.

Terry Brindle, *Yorkshire Post*: 'If resilience, determination and sheer fighting spirit can win championships, when form and fluency has been drained, then Leeds United will wrest the League title from Liverpool in ten days' time. Leeds's victory, amid the high drama of Bramall Lane last night, was a triumph for endeavour over the frustrations and threatening disappointment of a strangely contrasting season. It was a triumph for the commitment and character which keeps Leeds going long after bone and muscle ought to have rebelled… against never-ending pressure.'

The abiding memory for Brindle was Mick Jones' performance. Revie also was delighted with his centre forward. 'He did a tremendous job out there and worked unselfishly as always, and contributed so much. He hasn't been able to train since February but we've had to take a chance on him. Now treatment will start to get him fit for our next match against Ipswich.'

The clash against Ipswich was not for the faint-hearted and there was a fair amount of nail biting from Leeds supporters.

We started really well and took a two-goal lead, which settled everyone's nerves, but we let them back into the match. When they equalised you could sense the tension building, but we persevered and Allan scored a crucial goal to win the game for us. In the dressing room afterwards we felt a great sense of relief because we knew a draw in our final game would clinch the title.

After the game Revie admitted that after Ipswich equalised he thought, 'Oh no, it's going to happen to us again'. In the end though, everything worked out. However, Revie wasn't celebrating just yet. 'It's a bit premature to call us Champions. I'll not breathe easily until I see the trophy in Billy Bremner's hands.' Barry Foster of the *Yorkshire Post* summarised everyone's feelings. 'Almost there. That is how Leeds United must feel this morning… the odds on Leeds taking their second League title swung very heavily towards Elland Road.'

Our win over Ipswich placed enormous pressure on Liverpool. A few days later they played against Arsenal and finally cracked, losing 1-0. We were Champions again. Allan was round at my house that evening; when we heard the result we were ecstatic.

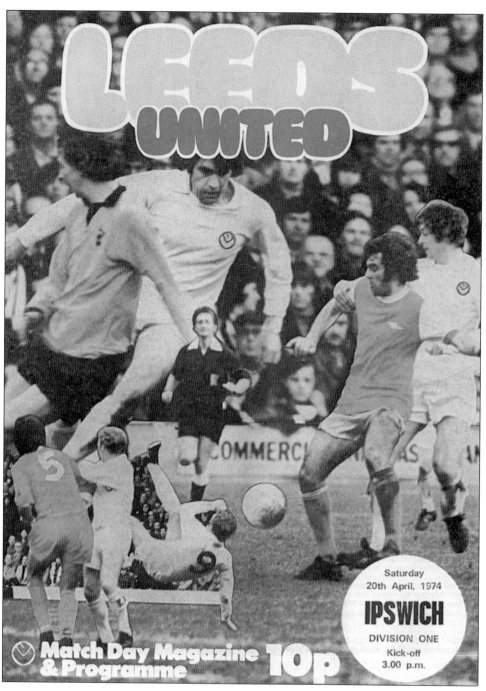

Mick's last match for Leeds United.

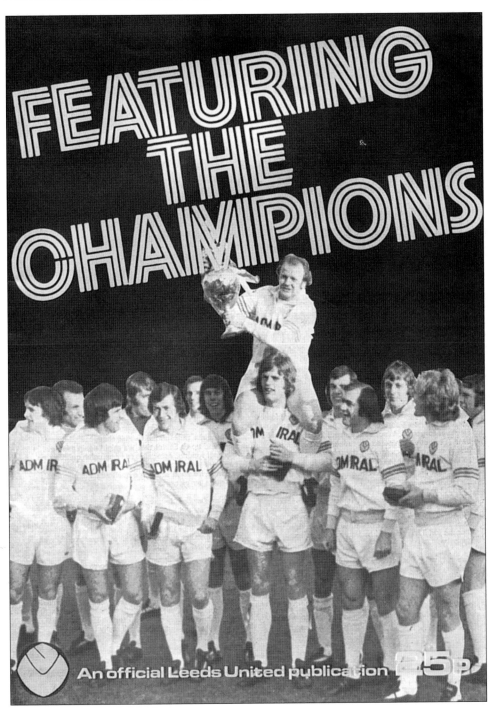

Champions.

Following Liverpool's defeat, Don Revie thought this triumph was the greatest achievement during his thirteen years as manager. 'When we won the First Division title last time we were able to keep a more settled formation. This season we have had to overcome a tremendous amount of switching about because we have had so many injury set-backs. It speaks volumes for the players who have come into the side and helped us so well that we have been able to win the title. They have worked tremendously hard throughout the season and I feel they have deserved the reward, which has now come their way. I am proud of them all.'

It was a close thing in the end, but I've always felt that if we hadn't picked up so many injuries to a number of players we'd have gone through the campaign undefeated as Don predicted we could pre-season. With the Championship settled I missed the last game of the season at QPR, which we won 1-0. Once again we'd proved we were the best around.

It was a bittersweet end to the season for me. I'd won my second championship medal, been voted Player of the Year by supporters and finished the campaign top-scorer for a third time. However, there was something radically wrong with my left knee.

Leeds United, First Division Champions 1973/74. From left to right, back row: McQueen, Stewart, Harvey, Ellam, Jordan, Clarke, Hunter, Madeley, Jones. Front row: Gray E., Lorimer, Yorath, Cherry, Reaney, Gray F., Cooper, Bates, Bremner.

Left: Simply the best. Right: Double champ!

Leeds United League record: P42 W 24 D 14 L 4 F 66 A 31 Pts 62

Player appearances during the season (substitute in brackets): Harvey 39; Reaney 36; Cherry 37 (1); Bremner 42; McQueen 36; Hunter 42; Lorimer 37; Clarke 34; Jones 28 (3); Giles 17; Madeley 39; Jordan 25 (8); Yorath 23 (5); Gray E 8; Bates 9 (1); Gray F 3 (3); Ellam 3 (1); Cooper (1) 1; Stewart 3; Liddell (1)

Goals: Jones 14; Clarke 13; Lorimer 12; Bremner 10; Jordan 7; Madeley 2; Giles 2; Yorath 2; Bates 2; Cherry 1; Own Goal 1.

The campaign was Don's last at the club. Like all the lads, over the years I'd grown close to him and it was a big disappointment when he decided to take the England job. I'd played under him for seven seasons and won all my major honours. Our consistency had been unbelievable. We'd been Champions twice and runners-up on three occasions. In addition, during this period we'd reached three FA Cup finals and three European finals, which was a record that no English team could match. It was obvious though that the great team was beginning to break up and I think this was one of the major reasons why he took the job during the close season. We all realised that the Revie era was over.

12

END OF THE ROAD
1974/75

During the close season a new manager arrived at Elland Road, and Mick began the long road back to fitness… or so he thought.

When Don left there was turmoil at the club. Brian Clough was appointed manager, which surprised a lot of the squad. He didn't have a great reputation with us because of the criticism he'd given the club down the years. On his first day he arranged a meeting with the whole squad in the players' lounge.

He spoke to each player; eventually he came to Eddie Gray. Eddie had a thigh problem – he'd had it since being a kid and always warmed up before us, whether for training or a game. When fit he was brilliant, as good as George Best in his prime; he had so much skill, but he had suffered spells out through injury. Brian told Eddie if he had been a racehorse he'd have been shot years ago. We could not believe it. Whether he did it as a joke I don't know, but at that moment he lost the squad's respect.

We'd developed an incredible team spirit over the years; there was no way we could play for him. I respected him as a manager, because he'd been successful, but he was the wrong manager at that time for Leeds United. Jimmy Armfield came in and was the complete opposite. He was quieter, encouraged us and certainly brought stability.

The club was determined to sort my knee out. I went to specialists all over the country but nobody knew what the problem was; X-rays revealed nothing. If you had a ligament or cartilage injury, you generally knew you'd get better, but this was puzzling everyone so naturally it concerned me a lot. I was still only twenty-eight and thought that I had years of playing ahead of me. Eventually Doc Adams recommended me to an orthopaedic specialist in Leeds, who decided an exploratory operation was necessary to find out once and for all what the problem was. I was relieved because finally I'd get some answers.

After the operation, he came to see me and told me he had found the problem. Some of the bone under the kneecap had flaked away. He'd cleaned it up, but it was fifty-fifty if I could play professionally again because it wasn't the type of injury that would

Recuperating at home with Mark and Lindsey.

heal. I was naturally upset, but at least I knew what I was dealing with. Whilst in hospital I missed the supporters club Player of the Year award at the Griffin Hotel, so Allan accepted the honour on my behalf.

Throughout my rehabilitation, I had a lot of physiotherapy at St James Hospital and spent months at Elland Road on my own trying to get fit. It was depressing at times; the worst part was missing the crack and banter of the dressing room. I did regain some of my fitness and played a few reserve matches, but only got about seventy per cent fit. Whereas I used to be able to climb high for headers, I couldn't anymore, and whenever I turned sharply, my knee still hurt. Deep down I realised that I was finished at the top level.

During the 1974/75 campaign, whilst I was trying to regain my fitness, the players overcame the managerial changes and behind-the-scenes problems to reach the European Cup final. I watched the match from the bench that night and could not believe they lost the final. The referee made some atrocious decisions. Beckenbauer brought down Allan for a blatant penalty and as for Peter's disallowed goal, I thought the decision by the referee was very harsh. During the close season it was obvious to me that the Leeds United I joined in 1967 was changing. Jack had retired, Terry Cooper had moved on, and Billy, Norman and John were approaching the end of their Leeds careers.

Back in action for the reserves ... alas it was not to be.

Mick Jones, 1994.

I could have played at a lower level, but my philosophy was always to aim for the top and finish there. I'd seen many great players play on when they clearly should not have, which I always thought was very sad. I was determined not to do that. Unfortunately for me, it was at a young age. I wanted to be remembered for the player I was; it was time to move on. I stopped going in to training and eventually retired in October 1975.

Following my retirement, initially I had no idea what I was going to do. I was twenty-nine, had no academic qualifications and being a footballer I'd had everything arranged for me. I was now on my own. It was time to get on with my life. I decided to stay within the sports industry and eventually got a job as a sales representative for Sondico Sports, which I enjoyed.

By 1982 though I'd had enough of the travelling. I'd done so much over the years; I just wanted a base. When a shop came available in Maltby, it was the perfect opportunity to move on. I ran Mick Jones Sports Ltd for fourteen years, before selling sports goods on the markets for a while.

Glenis and I have been very fortunate because our children have always lived nearby, and we like nothing more than spending time with them and our grandchildren. Mark is married to Serena; they have two children, Shelley and

The Jones family, 2002.

Mason, and our daughter Lindsey is married to David. Naturally, I still look out for the scores of Sheffield United and Leeds United.

I may have had to retire early, but I have no regrets. I was fortunate to begin my professional career at a club where I had the chance to break into top-flight football as a teenager, and then move on to a club that developed into the most consistent team in England. At Leeds, I played in a team full of international players and achieved all the ambitions I set myself when I dreamed of being a professional footballer.

LEEDS UNITED
'DREAM SQUAD'

When I began my professional football career, I played with a number of talented footballers at Sheffield United. However, during my peak years as a player I was fortunate to play in a team that has become acknowledged as one of the greatest of the post-war era.

David Harvey was a top class goalkeeper. A great professional, you could find few faults with him. A terrific shot-stopper, brave, commanding in his penalty area, David made some wonderful saves over the years. Though ability-wise there was not a lot to choose between him and Gary Sprake, I always felt more comfortable when he was in goal. Throughout a game he'd watch every move on the pitch, wherever the ball was, his concentration was superb. A Scottish international, he was their first choice in the mid-seventies and was voted the outstanding goalkeeper of the 1974 World Cup by the world's press – some accolade!

Paul Reaney was a superb right-back and unbelievably quick. He had great pace going down the line when either supporting the attack or getting back to defend. A solid tackler and fitness fanatic, George Best used to hate playing against him because he never got a kick. His positional sense and reading of a game got us out of trouble on many occasions, especially with his numerous goal line clearances. He was not a flamboyant type of player; he went out and did his job. An England international, but for his broken leg he'd have gone to the 1970 World Cup finals.

Terry Cooper was the best left-back around when I played, and linked up brilliantly with Eddie Gray. A solid tackler, he occasionally got caught out when someone came at him quickly, but he was some player when attacking defenders; he added tremendous width to the side. Terry started as a left-winger; so coming forward was natural for him. His close control and ability to keep possession was superb. Unfortunately, a broken leg in 1972 not only cost him his cup final spot, but his place in the Leeds side long term. He was an England regular for a number of years, and his performances in the 1970 World Cup gained him world-class status.

Billy Bremner was a winner, simple as that. Determined, enthusiastic and a battler, he was different to John Giles, but what a partnership they formed in midfield. He also scored so many important goals for a midfield player. Billy had so much ability, many a time he joined the attack with devastating effect; he could have played anywhere. He may have been temperamental, but that was because of his will to win; he was undoubtedly a world-class footballer. Billy Bremner was the dressing room; he was at the centre of everything both on and off the pitch. Scotland's skipper for many years, he led them superbly in the 1974 World Cup finals. His death hit all the players hard, and he's sadly missed.

Jack Charlton was a tremendous centre half. He was a bit older than the rest of us but was a key member of the team. During the early 1960s, Jack was an ordinary footballer, but Don Revie made him into the player he was. Unbeatable in the air, as a defender he did a great job and was one of the best around. It was almost impossible to get round those long legs of his and he scored so many goals for us, it was incredible. From set pieces he was always dangerous. A stalwart for England, Jack was a star in the 1966 World Cup finals.

Norman Hunter was a tremendous professional. I played against him in my early years and was delighted to be on his side. His tackling was ferocious and gained him the nickname Norman 'bites yer legs', but although he was genuinely hard, there was never any intent. Norman had a great left foot and could pass the ball any distance. He had superb positional sense and was strong in the air. One of the best defenders around, but for Bobby Moore he would have won a lot more caps for England. Norman was such a winner and so determined, when we went out his desire was unbelievable.

Peter Lorimer was the youngest player to represent Leeds United and, in my opinion, underestimated as a footballer. Of course, he'll always be remembered for his shooting ability but he had a lot more to his game than that. He was very skilful, had great balance and could cross the ball with tremendous accuracy. He was also incredibly confident; he always believed he'd score in every game. The number of goals 'hot-shot' Lorimer scored was sensational, especially when you consider he played on the right wing, not as a central striker. I lost count of the goals I scored as a result of goalkeepers being unable to handle his shots. Still Leeds United's record goal scorer, he represented Scotland on many occasions, including the 1974 World Cup finals.

Allan Clarke was the most clinical goalscorer around when one on one with a goalkeeper; he was lethal. When Allan and a goalkeeper faced each other, we could safely turn around and walk back! Allan was up there with the likes of Hurst, Greaves and Law as a finisher. Allan was supremely confident, superb in the air and worked really hard for the benefit of the team. Our partnership was the best I experienced as a player; it's just a shame we were not given the opportunity to represent England together. Allan showed his temperament and pedigree when he scored a penalty on his England debut in the 1970 World Cup finals. Don was spot on when he paired us together.

John Giles was the best footballer I played with. Creative and a clinical passer of the ball, John could destroy opponents with one pass. He had two great feet, could pass a ball over any distance and like Billy scored a tremendous number of goals. A master tactician and reader of a game he was superb at spreading play. He developed a telepathic understanding with Billy. As a combination, they became one of the most feared in Europe. His accuracy made him a natural penalty taker and he rarely missed. He also had a mean streak in him, which he didn't need because he was so skilful, but he could dish it out! We were all dedicated, but John was easily the most disciplined player I've known. A regular for the Republic of Ireland for years, John was a brilliant footballer.

Eddie Gray was a sensational player. He was so skilful, his solo-effort against Burnley in 1970 was just incredible, and easily the best goal I've ever witnessed. Eddie went past players as if they weren't there, a quick shimmy and he was gone. His dribbling skills were unbelievable; at times defenders simply didn't know what to do. He could go either side of them, and if they dived in he was past them in a flash. Unfortunately for Eddie, he missed many games due to injury, which also limited his appearances for Scotland. When fit though he was unstoppable, as he demonstrated against Chelsea in the 1970 FA Cup final at Wembley. Eddie was as skilful as George Best was, and but for injuries would have been acknowledged as one of the greatest wingers of all time.

Paul Madeley would have got in any world side. To be able to slot into the team at a moment's notice and play with such consistency was incredible. He offered so much flexibility and played in every position but goalkeeper. If someone was injured during a game, we could soon adjust; Paul never moaned, he simply got on with it. He was a sensational talent. My room-mate for many years, Paul could play anywhere with ease, although striker was not his favoured spot. Probably his best position was in defence or in a defensive midfield role, but such was his ability, when he deputised for someone they normally only got back in when another player was injured! An England international for many years, Paul was the greatest all-round footballer I played with.

As for myself, as a member of this squad, I would like to thank Elsie Revie and a number of my former colleagues for their kind words.

Elsie Revie: Don thought that Mick Jones was a great professional. Mick was the salt of the earth and a player who would always give one hundred per cent every time he went on the field. He knew the sort of game he was going to give and what he was going to do. He was a manager's dream. Mick Jones was a great centre forward and was definitely one of the backbones of Leeds United.

Peter Lorimer: Playing with Mick Jones was a pleasure. Being a wide player, when I got in trouble I needed someone to help me out, and I always knew that if I swung the ball to the far post, Mick would be there to win the ball for me. He was one of these guys that was an unsung hero, and never really received the acclaim he should have received. Although he never scored as many goals as 'Sniffer' Clarke and myself, he was probably responsible for us scoring more goals than anyone else. That said, he scored some terrific goals and was a fantastic player.

John Giles: Mick Jones was a terrific lad, very honest and always gave everything in a game. He was exceptionally modest, never thought of himself and had great ability as a footballer.

Mick had a lot of skill but it was his honesty that shone for me. If he made a mistake it was an honest one, and for me he was worth his weight in gold for Leeds United. His partnership with Allan Clarke was ideal. Allan would normally come for the ball and get it to his feet, whereas Mick was prepared to go behind people and he scored a lot of vital goals for us. He had great character and it was a pleasure to play with him. He couldn't help but give everything when he played. I have the highest admiration for him.

Norman Hunter: How Mick didn't lose his temper a bit more I don't know. After the '72 cup final, if we'd had Mick Jones on the Monday night against Wolves we'd have won the title and the double. For me, so long as Mick was on the team sheet I was satisfied. My role was to get the ball and give it to Billy and Johnny, if I didn't I'd play it long to Jonah, and nine times out of ten I knew that he would be on the end of it. I played against him in his Sheffield United days, and he scored against me. The ball was played in and he stuck it away in the bottom corner; I wasn't happy. Even though not a 'natural' goal scorer, Mick was a great player, and in all the years I played the game nobody played with a bigger heart than Mick Jones. Clarkie scored goals, but he would not have scored as many without Mick. He was a brilliant signing.

Paul Madeley: Mick Jones was my room-mate for many years. Mick scored a lot of goals for Leeds, but the one that always springs to mind was the one he scored against Chelsea in the replay at Old Trafford, it put us one-up and was an absolute cracker. The other notable memory was his injury in the cup final against Arsenal a couple of years later. I'll always remember looking up into the Royal Box when he was determined to receive his medal from the Queen. Mick was a most unselfish player, and a team man. He was always more concerned that the team would do well rather than taking the glory himself. He was a great player to play with.

The last word on Mick comes from his strike partner Allan Clarke: Mick was a bit like the older style centre forward. He was the target man. Normally it takes a season for a partnership to gel, but Mick and I, although he doesn't think so, hit it off immediately because I was a different type of striker to him. Mick was such an honest player and would chase lost causes, that was his nature and it made a fantastic partnership. Mick had terrific close control and used his strength to hold the ball up while I looked for space to support him. If I was being man-marked I'd go deeper to pick balls up. Any crosses that came into the box one of us would attack the near post; the other would peel off to the back-stick. He was a brilliant header of the ball and scored his fair share of goals. We were compared to Toshack and Keegan of Liverpool, Radford and Kennedy of Arsenal, Chivers and Gilzean of Tottenham, and Osgood and Baldwin of Chelsea. None of them touched us! My only regret was that we didn't represent England together. When you think that we were probably the most feared partnership in Europe, it's unbelievable. He was certainly the best striker I played with.

Club	Season	League Division	League Apps	League Goals	League Position	FA Cup Apps	FA Cup Goals	FA Cup Round	L Cup Apps	L Cup Goals	L Cup Round	Europe Apps	Europe Goals	Europe Round	Ch Sld Apps	Other Goals	Total Apps	Total Goals	Top Scorer
Sheffield United	1962/63	One	6	4	10	-	-	5	-	-	3	-	-	-	-	-	6	4	
Sheffield United	1963/64	One	23	5	12	3	3	4	-	-	2	-	-	-	-	-	26	8	
Sheffield United	1964/65	One	39	14	19	3	3	4	1	-	2	-	-	-	-	-	43	17	*
Sheffield United	1965/66	One	40	21	9	1	-	4	1	-	2	-	-	-	-	-	42	21	*
Sheffield United	1966/67	One	33	15	10	4	3	5	4	1	Q/F	-	-	-	-	-	41	19	*
Sheffield United	1967/68	One	8	4	21	-	-	Q/F	1	-	2	-	-	-	-	-	9	4	
Summary			**149**	**63**		**11**	**9**		**7**	**1**		**-**	**-**		**-**	**-**	**167**	**73**	
Leeds United	1967/68	One	25	8	4	5	2	SF	-	-	W	8	2	W	-	-	38	12	
Leeds United	1968/69	One	40	14	1	2	-	3	3	2	4	8	1	Q/F	-	-	53	17	
Leeds United	1969/70	One	32	15	2	9	3	F	3	-	3	8	8	S/F	1	-	53	26	*
Leeds United	1970/71	One	39	6	2	3	3	5	1	-	2	9	1	W	-	-	52	10	*
Leeds United	1971/72	One	24	11	2	5	2	W	1	-	3	-	-	1	-	-	30	13	
Leeds United	1972/73	One	27(1)	9	3	8	1	F	4(1)	3	4	6	3	F	-	-	45(2)	16	
Leeds United	1973/74	One	28(3)	14	1	4	1	5	1	-	2	3	2	3	-	-	36(3)	17	*
Summary			**215(4)**	**77**		**36**	**12**		**13(1)**	**5**		**42**	**17**		**1**	**-**	**305/5**	**111**	*

Debut games

Club	Opposition	Competition	Date	Result
Sheffield United	Manchester United	Division One	20-Apr-63	1-1
Leeds United	Leicester City	Division One	23-Sep-67	3-2

Debut goals

Club	Opposition	Competition	Date	Result	Goals
Sheffield United	Manchester City	Division One	24-Apr-63	3-1	2
Sheffield United	Lincoln City	FA Cup	4-Jan-64	4-0	2
Sheffield United	Burnley	League Cup	5-Oct-66	2-0	1
Leeds United	Arsenal	Division One	4-Nov-67	3-1	1
Leeds United	Nottingham Forest	FA Cup	17-Feb-68	2-1	1
Leeds United	Charlton Athletic	League Cup	4-Sep-68	1-0	1
Leeds United	Lyn Oslo	European Cup	17-Sep-69	10-0	3
Leeds United	Ankaraguca	European Cup Winners Cup	27-Sep-72	1-0	1
Leeds United	Spora Luxembourg	Fairs Cup	3-Oct-67	9-0	1

Hat-Tricks

Club	Opposition	Competition	Date	Result	Goals
Leeds United	Lyn Oslo	European Cup	17-Sep-69	10-0	3
Leeds United	Swindon Town	FA Cup	23-Jan-71	4-0	3
Leeds United	Manchester United	Division One	19-Feb-72	5-1	3

INTERNATIONAL PLAYING CAREER

Level	Date	Competition	Opposition	Venue	Score	Goals	Attendance
England Under-23	25-Nov-64	Friendly	Rumania Under-23	Highfield Road, Coventry City	5-0	1	27,476
England Under-23	24-Feb-65	Friendly	Scotland Under-23	Pittodrie, Aberdeen	0-0	-	25,000
England Under-23	7-Apr-65	Friendly	Czechoslovakia Under-23	Elland Road, Leeds United	0-0	-	8,533
England Under-23	25-May-65	Friendly	West Germany Under-23	Freiburg	0-1	-	15,000
England Under-23	2-Jun-65	Friendly	Austria Under-23	Vienna	0-0	-	
England Under-23	3-Nov-65	Friendly	France Under-23	Carrow Road, Norwich City	3-0	2	20,203
England Under-23	24-Nov-65	Friendly	Yugoslavia Under-23	The Dell, Southampton	2-1	1	23,035
England Under-23	20-Apr-66	Friendly	Turkey Under-23	Ewood Park, Blackburn Rovers	2-0	-	9,251
England Under-23	10-May-67	Friendly	Austria Under-23	Bootferry Park, Hull City	3-0	-	
Young England	30-Apr-65	Friendly	England	Highbury, Arsenal	2-2	-	26,840
England	12-May-65	Friendly	West Germany	Nurembourg	1-0	-	69,000
England	16-May-65	Friendly	Sweden	Gothenburg	2-1	-	18,000
England	14-Jan-70	Friendly	Holland	Wembley	0-0	-	75,000